Political and Social Economy Series
Edited by C. Addison Hickman and Michael P. Shields

Other Books in This Series:

Randall G. Holcombe

PUBLIC FINANCE
AND THE
POLITICAL PROCESS

Southern Illinois University Press
Carbondale and Edwardsville

LIBRARY OF CONGRESS CATALOGING IN PUBLICATION DATA

Holcombe, Randall G.
   Public finance and the political process.

   (Political and social economy series)
   Bibliography: p.
   Includes index.
   1.   Finance, Public—Decision making.   2.   Public
administration—Decision making.   3.   Political par-
ticipation.   I.   Title.   II.   Series.
HJ141.H57   1983   350.72   82-10803
ISBN 0-8093-1082-1

To my father

CONTENTS

TABLES

FIGURES

PREFACE

The main purpose of this book is to examine the decision-making process in the public sector of a democracy—the process through which the preferences of voters are translated into public sector output. The process is complex, and although a great deal is understood about it, there is still a great deal left to learn. I hope this book will be able to contribute something to that body of knowledge.

Many of the ideas developed in this book have appeared already in journal articles, but I thought it worthwhile to include them in a book for two main reasons. First, it has provided me the opportunity to expand upon and refine my earlier ideas. More significantly, though, presenting these ideas in book form has enabled me to relate many ideas together, and, I hope, to present them as a coherent whole, rather than as isolated pictures of specific aspects of public sector activity. The result is intended to give the reader a general model of the way in which individual preferences are aggregated in order to produce the demand for public sector output.

The ideas in this book have been developed over a number of years, and have been influenced by a number of people. Foremost on the list is James M. Buchanan, under whom I had the good fortune of studying as a graduate student. His influence is evident in the subject matter and approach that I have used (and also in my many references to his work). In addition, he has provided many helpful comments on parts of the manuscript. Gordon Tullock also deserves significant mention for his influence on my thinking, as well as the many comments that he has provided on portions of the manuscript.

Many other people have had an impact on the contents of this book. Chapter 9 was written after I had heard a series of lectures by Robert Summers, and the legal cases cited there were selected from those that he discussed. Some of the material in chapters 5 and 7 is from articles coauthored with Mark Crain, Edward Price, Paul Taylor, and Robert Tollison. In addition, Robert Tollison also provided helpful comments on other material in the manuscript. Other individuals whose ideas have found their way into the book include Ronald Batchelder, Robert Ekelund, Richard Higgins, and Mack Ott. I am most grateful for the insights of all of these individuals, but since none of them saw the manuscript in its entirety, the usual disclaimer is especially appropriate, and they should not be held accountable for the book's shortcomings.

Some of the material in this book has been developed from previously published material, and I gratefully acknowledge the *Atlantic Economic Journal, Economic Inquiry, National Tax Journal, Public Choice,* and *Public Finance Quarterly* for allowing me to use material for the book. The manuscript was typed at the Manuscript Preparation Center at the School of Business, Auburn University, and Bess Yellen deserves more than the customary credit for efficiently overseeing the production of the manuscript. In addition, parts of the manuscript were typed by Delores Nunez, Gail Micsinszki, and Loraine Hyde. Their efficiency has made my job in preparing the manuscript considerably easier.

I am also grateful to the Earhart Foundation for providing financial support for part of this project. Its support enabled me to devote more time to the preparation of the manuscript than I otherwise would have found possible.

To avoid cumbersome language, I have employed masculine nouns and pronouns in places where there are no simple descriptive nouns or pronouns in English to denote both genders. This was done only to simplify the writing style.

RANDALL G. HOLCOMBE

Auburn, Alabama
February 1983

1

Introduction

The years since World War II have seen important changes in the way in which economists have analyzed public policy measures.[1] Historical events, no doubt, have influenced the evolution of economic analysis, for it was not the basic theory or techniques of economics that changed, but rather the specific types of public policy issues that were being evaluated in the academic literature. At the beginning of the 1950s, the onset of the Great Depression was only twenty years in the past, and Keynes's very successful *General Theory* was less than fifteen years old.[2] The classical economists, as Keynes had called them, had a tradition dating back to Adam Smith of defending the unfettered market as the best means for allocating economic resources. As the Great Depression cast doubt upon the classical theory, Keynes explained how an economy could remain in an underemployment equilibrium, and more significantly, proposed how the government might intervene in order to remedy the situation. The world economy did not really recover from the depression until World War II, which brought with it the increased government expenditures and government budget deficits that Keynesian theory had prescribed. Economists no longer had to be content merely to explain the operation of a market economy and extol the virtues of free trade. They now had a more powerful theory to describe how, during times when the market failed to provide full employment, the government could intervene in order to correct the shortcomings of the market.[3]

Economists at least since the time of Pigou had rigorously analyzed other types of market failure,[4] but the success of the theory of aggregate demand management prompted a renewed interest in the theory of market failure and the implied prescriptions for governmental action to remedy the problems.[5] The analysis of market failure is an exciting area of research because the observation that actual markets do not work as well as ideal markets carries with it the implication that some type of intervention could improve the operation of the market. The economist who has studied an aspect of market failure is likely to be in the best position to be the social engineer who designs the remedy. Because of the way in which market failure has been analyzed in the literature, obvious solutions have suggested themselves. Corrective taxes are called for in the case of externalties, and collective provision is implied for public goods. While some cases of market failure are primarily dealt with in macroeconomics or industrial organization, the most rapidly developing areas naturally fall in the area of public finance. The most frequently suggested solutions to these problems of market failure generally involve taxation or public sector spending, which itself implies taxation. Hence the appearance of the term "public finance" in the title of this book.

In its early stages, very naïve solutions were proposed to problems of market failure. If the market was shown to "fail," the term meaning not to act as an ideal market, then the solution was to inform the government of the optimal result and turn the problem over to the public sector. Knowing what would be best, the government could then either regulate the market or take over production itself. But markets were shown to fail because individuals were shown not to have the proper incentives to produce optimally. Presumably, simply informing market participants of the optimal results that are desired would not generate an optimal result, although it was frequently implied that the government would produce optimal results once the desired results were known. Real-world markets were being compared with ideal governments.

This situation prompted public finance economists to examine the institutional structure of the public sector using the same tools of economic analysis that were being used to examine the private sector, giving birth to the subdiscipline of public choice. Public choice uses economic analysis to describe political institutions.[6] Now, public sector institutions are analyzed in the same way as private sector institutions, recognizing that individuals in the public sector respond to incentives in the same way as individuals in the private sector. Incentives implied in the institutional structure of the public sector may or may not lead to optimal behavior on the part of the government. Public sector decisions take place through the political process, which begins in a democracy with the voters. Voters elect representatives, who have the incentive to be reelected in order to keep their jobs, and the bureaucrats who carry out public policy face incentives also. As in the private sector of the economy, sometimes individuals in the public sector have an incentive to act in the public interest, and sometimes they do not. In order to understand how the activities of public finance will actually be carried out by the government, the political process must be analyzed. Hence the appearance of the term "political process" in the title of this book.

This evolution in the way in which public sector institutions are analyzed by economists has provided a more balanced approach in evaluating public policy. A theory of government failure has been developing to parallel the theory of market failure, so that when markets do not provide optimal resource allocation, turning the problem over to government is no longer automatically suggested. Instead, the efficiency of the market must be compared with the efficiency of the government. Applied to the public sector, economic theory allows public sector resource allocation to be evaluated on the same terms as private sector resource allocation. This is the purpose of studying public finance and the political process.

Years ago, Keynes noted in the *General Theory* that "the ideas of economists and political philosophers, both when they are right and when they are wrong, are more powerful than is commonly understood. Indeed the world is ruled by little else. Practical men, who believe themselves to be quite exempt from any intellectual influences, are usually the slaves of some defunct economist."[7] Keynes was certainly prophetic in his own case, and if his statement is generally true, then the development of ideas concerning economic and political philosophy is important. Ideas matter.

Although the theory of resource allocation in the private sector has been studied extensively, relatively little work has been done to explore resource allocation through the public sector. That situation is rapidly changing, and much of the new work on resource allocation through the public sector illustrates that there are significant problems involved using the public sector to allocate resources efficiently. An understanding of the political decision-making process is necessary in order to see both the abilities and the limitations of resource allocation through the public sector, and that is a primary purpose of this work. This study of public finance and the political process is intended to examine some aspects of the way in which the public sector allocates economic resources. The institution of voting plays a central role, and will be discussed at length. Related topics of the philosophical foundations of the political system, the development of the legal structure, and theoretical concepts of equilibrium in the public sector are also covered in separate chapters. The central purpose of this study, to emphasize, is to increase understanding of the abilities and limitations of public sector decision making.

The advantages of discovering the abilities of public sector decision making are obvious, but especially in the political climate of the twentieth century, a clear understanding of the limitations of public sector decision making may be more valuable. The New Deal of the 1930s began an era where anytime a problem with the society was identified, asking the government to initiate a new program to deal with that problem was accepted as a legitimate solution. Political slogans often have a hollow ring. For example, looking back, some people might not feel that the Great Society of Lyndon Johnson was all that great; but nobody can deny that, for better or for worse, the New Deal was really a new deal. As a result, government activity has mushroomed as the government has become an accepted party in all kinds of activities that would have before been considered outside the government's legitimate domain.

Consequently, there is now much more room for diverse opinions about what the government should be doing than before, simply because individuals have diverse goals. While the question of what the government should be doing appears to be a strictly normative question, there is more of a positive element involved than is commonly realized, and many questions may in fact be strictly positive. In looking at the limitations of governmental activity, many of the goals that individuals might like to achieve through the public sector might in fact not be attainable. The policy question is then placed in positive terms: is the attainment of this goal in the opportunity set? Many disputes that appear on the surface to be normative are in fact positive questions about the nature of the opportunity set.

Even this argument probably understates the case since, ultimately, most people share most of the same social goals. Most people would express a preference for eliminating poverty, improving education and public health, protecting individual rights, and living in a prosperous society with a high standard of living. The disagreement comes over what the best means are for achieving those goals. Some will favor more reliance on private enterprise while others favor a larger role for the government, but this is largely a positive question about what the best means are for achieving the goals that are generally held. Many policy questions that appear to be normative are really positive disputes about the nature of the opportunity set that faces the society.[8] Herein lies the benefits of understanding the limitations of governmental activity. If the true nature of the choices facing society is agreed upon, there will be far fewer disputes about the proper role of government, since ultimate social goals are held more in common than opinions about the potential effectiveness of public sector institutions in specific situations.

Outline of Chapters

The chapters to follow will largely be concerned with the capability of public sector institutions to allocate resources efficiently. There is heavy emphasis placed upon majority rule voting, especially in the first two-thirds of the book. Later, the philosophical foundations of a liberal society are examined within a contractarian framework, and the development of the common law is analyzed, since the common law is at the foundation of society's legal structure.

The analysis in the next chapter will begin by discussing a number of concepts of public sector equilibrium. These concepts are frequently discussed in the public finance literature, and chapter 2 takes the familiar concepts and analyzes them all within a common framework. This way the relationships between the many concepts can all be clearly seen and analyzed. Chapter 2 goes on to discuss the implications and uses of the various concepts as well. Chapter 2 provides a foundation for the rest of the book by analyzing, defining, and discusssing the relevance of the various concepts of public sector equilibrium, concentrating especially on the political implications of these ideas. A key concept in analyzing political processes is the concept of Bowen equilibrium. Bowen equilibrium results from a majority rule political setting, providing certain assumptions are met, so the concept of Bowen equilibrium will be important throughout the book.

Directly related to the concept of Bowen equilibrium is the possibility of agenda control in the public sector. Agenda control is the topic of chapter 3. The way that Bowen and others have modeled decision making under majority rule, the outcome most preferred by the median voter is selected under majority rule politics. The relatively recent literature on agenda control works within the median voter model, but concludes that majority rule politics will result in a larger level of expenditures than would be most preferred by the median voter. This result is dependent upon two major assumptions. The government officials who control the agenda must desire a level of expenditures larger than the level most preferred by the median voter, and those officials must also be able to control the items on the agenda from which the voters may select. Using the same basic institutional structure and voter behavior as the Bowen model, the agenda control literature concludes that expenditures will be above Bowen equilibrium.

Chapter 4 empirically tests the median voter model by comparing the results predicted by the standard model with the results predicted by the agenda control model developed in chapter 3. The empirical test uses data from school districts in Michigan, and for this data set the empirical test supports the Bowen model rather than the agenda control model. Other empirical tests in the literature are described, and the chapter speculates about the generality of the results.

Public sector institutions seem to be designed so that under ideal conditions Bowen equilibrium will be produced. Chapter 5 describes the Florida system, a referendum system that will always produce Bowen equilibrium. The system is simple and straightforward, and could be used to replace all existing referendum systems. In addition, chapter 5 describes how the Florida system could be used as a national referendum for allocating the Federal budget, and even determining its size. In light of the fact that public sector institutions are generally designed to produce Bowen equilibrium under majority rule, and also in light of the doubt cast upon the ability of these institutions by models such as the agenda control model, a more widespread application of the Florida system would appear desirable.

The median voter model theme is continued in chapter 6, where a median voter model is developed in which candidates can propose variable tax shares as a part of their platforms. This model illustrates that when tax shares can be included in political platforms, there will be a tendency for government budgets to be larger than when tax shares are constitutionally given. This conclusion, formulated within the median voter model, directly follows from the law of demand. Competing parties will vie for the median voter's vote by lowering the median voter's tax share. A lower price per unit of government expenditures implies that the median voter will demand a larger amount of government output, so the public sector will increase in size.

Chapter 7 explores some elements of monopoly power in government. Some amount of monopoly power would be necessary for the agenda control model to operate as described in chapter 3, so chapter 7 explores the foundations of this monopoly power. In a majority rule system, political coalitions are essentially natural monopolies, since only one majority can exist at a time. The cost of producing legislation includes the fixed cost of forming the coalition, but the marginal cost of additional legislation to an established coalition is relatively small. Chapter 7 draws implications from this parallel, and also discusses monopoly aspects of governmental bureaucracies.

Chapter 8 uses a contractarian model to describe why a social contract establishing a liberal society would be likely to erode over time. When the contract is being negotiated in a society to have elected leaders, none of the negotiators knows who will be elected to political office. The contract will tend to be unbiased, at least in the sense that it will not favor the public sector over the private sector. Once the contract takes effect, elected officials are the only ones who can change the contract, so there will be a bias introduced in favor of the public sector. Over time, the public sector will gain more power and greater control over resources as the contract erodes.

The basic rules of society are established through the common law rather than explicitly through legislation, and chapter 9 describes how the common law develops. There is an invisible hand that guides the common law toward efficient rules in the same way that the market mechanism guides economic activity in an efficient direction. Developing an efficient general legal rule is more difficult than making an efficient decision in a particular case, and the common law develops general rules through a series of decisions in individual cases. Developing general rules on a case by case basis is therefore more likely to result in efficient rules. In addition, the broadening and narrowing of precedent allows efficient decisions to be reinforced while weeding out inefficient decisions. After chapter 9 deals with these aspects of the law, chapter 10 draws the work to a close with conclusions and implications.

Public Finance and the Political Process

The most fundamental issue to be examined when analyzing public finance and the political process is the issue of where the state obtains the authority to tax its citizens and then determine how those revenues are used. At one extreme, the state could be viewed as a totalitarian tyrant whose authority is grounded in force. Coercion is the sole source of authority in this view, but this extreme probably never has been a historical reality. Individuals would have nothing to lose by attempting to overthrow the tyrannical government. At the other extreme, the government might be viewed as a voluntary association of individuals—a sort of club—where its authority derives from the voluntary consent of its members.[9] In actuality, all governments throughout history have probably been some combination of these extremes. There are undoubtedly collective benefits to be realized when the entire society organizes in order to pursue some activities. The protection of individual rights is probably the most obvious example, and even the most totalitarian government has provided a degree of protection to its citizens, both from aggression from inside and outside the society, as long as those citizens obeyed the rules of the government.[10]

The collective benefits of government produce consumer surplus for its citizens, and since governments are in general monopoly providers of at least some services, they have the power to coerce in a manner similar to the tie-in sale of an economic monopolist. In order to receive consumer surplus from living in an orderly society—the order being produced by government—citizens must abide by the other conditions the government mandates.[11] Since any government ultimately rules by force, is there any way to justify the government's power as being legitimate? The social contract theory of the state is an attempt to answer this question affirmatively. The members of society have implicitly agreed to the terms of the social contract.

More details of this agreement are discussed in chapter 8, but the important thing to note here is that to the extent that the social contract theory is valid, every aspect of the political process is the result of voluntary exchange, and so is clearly subject to economic analysis at the most fundamental level. But even if the formation of the government is viewed as a voluntary exchange, elements of coercion still tend to emerge as time passes. The terms of the contract must be flexible enough to deal with nw and unforseen circumstances, but the only way that change can occur is through the government. This means that there will be an automatic bias favoring those in the government when new rules are made, since those in the government make the rules. Anyone outside of government who wants to have the power to change the rules of society must be elected into the government, so even though there may be competition for the office of rule maker, there will not be competition between rules favoring those in the private sector and rules favoring those in the public sector.

Although these legislated rules are important for determining the course that a society follows, most social rules are generated through common law rather than statutory law. Chapter 9 examines the common law process, so although chapters 8 and 9 appear at the end of the book, they discuss the foundations of the social structure upon which public finance and the political process is built. The first seven chapters take the social structure analyzed in chapters 8 and 9 as given.

The most important political institution in a democracy is the election, and so the emphasis of the following analysis is on majority rule voting. Even though the underlying philosophy of majority rule voting is to produce the outcome preferred by the voters, majority rule elections can frequently distort this outcome, so that a majority rule outcome may not be representative of voter preferences. This is not to say that voters should be able to decide important matters regarding governmental decisions. For the most part, the subject of what decisions should reflect the preferences of the electorate and what decisions should be made by the best judgment of individuals in authority is ignored. The subject considered at length in the chapters below is that when decisions are supposedly made by voters through the election process, the outcomes may not be representative of voter preferences.

An important reason why this is so lies in the monopoly aspects of government, and the competition of candidates in a democracy for positions in the monopoly government. In competing for positions of power, candidates in a majority rule system must win the vote of the median voter. This leads candidates to compete for the median vote by offering to lower the median voter's tax share or raise the benefits accruing to the median voter if elected. The result is to cause the median voter's tax price per unit of governmental output to fall, implying a larger demand for output. The public sector grows as a result. Once elected, politicians are in a monopoly position and are able to increase the size of government by extracting some of the consumer surplus the government supplies. Even when referenda are held, the party that sets the agenda of a referendum has a great deal of control over the outcome.

A prerequisite for discussing the outcomes of elections and how closely the actual outcomes correspond with some ideal outcome is some notion of the types of outcomes that could be—or should be—produced in the public sector. Chapter 2 provides this foundation by discussing different concepts of public sector equilibrium.

Concepts of Public Sector Equilibrium

An appropriate starting point in the study of public finance and the political process is an examination of theories about how resources are, or should be, allocated in the public sector. Prior to World War II, the English language literature on public finance was primarily concerned with taxation, and important contributions concerning the theory of resource allocation through the public sector were not made until after that time.[1] Only after the English language literature began to develop were the important contributions by Lindahl and Wicksell—made considerably earlier—integrated into the literature. The introduction of these concepts of public sector equilibrium caused a significant change in the emphasis of the public finance literature. Before, taxes were considered in isolation, and a good tax was one which could raise revenue in as painless a way as possible. As the concepts of public sector equilibrium became a part of the public finance literature, taxes were more likely to be evaluated in conjunction with the expenditures they are supposed to finance. As a result of the change in emphasis, taxes are now analyzed as the price paid for public sector output.

In recent years, the micro-foundations of public finance theory have become increasingly more sophisticated, and a theory of resource allocation through the public sector is developing to parallel the well-established microeconomic theory describing resource allocation through the private sector. This sophistication has brought with it the development and use of a large number of concepts of public sector equilibrium. The purpose of this chapter is twofold. First, the chapter develops a theoretical comparison among several models of public sector equilibrium in order to show the theoretical relationship of one model to another. Second, the chapter describes the applicability of the various models to real-world institutional structures.

In order to compare the various concepts of public sector equilibrium, each will be examined within the same basic framework, using the simplest form of each model. While such a framework may obscure some of the elegance of the concepts and will make the description differ in some details from that of the original author, I hope these shortcomings will be outweighed by the advantage of being able to show clearly the relationships among the various equilibria. The framework in this chapter will be partial equilibrium with emphasis on the marginal conditions of each public sector equilibrium concept. Thus, there will be obvious differences between this framework and Samuelson's,[2] which is general equilibrium, and Lindahl's,[3] which emphasizes average rather than marginal tax rates.

In most cases, the origins of the particular concepts of public sector equilibrium can be traced to specific writers. This chapter will use that fact by referring to each concept by the name of its originator. This method of appellation should eliminate one potential source of confusion. For example, both of the familiar concepts of Samuelson equilibrium and of Lindahl equilibrium could be thought of as "public goods equilibria"; and like the Bowen equilibrium, the Niskanen equilibrium is also a type of median voter equilibrium.

The concepts to be described in this taxonomy are Samuelson equilibrium, Bowen equilibrium, Lindahl equilibrium and Wicksellian unanimity, Tiebout equilibrium, and Niskanen equilibrium. Probably the most widely referenced, and the first to be discussed here, is the Samuelson equilibrium.

Samuelson Equilibrium

In his pioneering articles on public goods, Paul Samuelson[4] defined a collective consumption good as one in which an additional individual's consumption of the good does not subtract from any other individuals' consumption; so that if the total amount of the good is represented by X, and individual i's consumption by X_i, then $X = X_i$ for all i. Representing individual i's marginal valuation for the good by V_i, and the marginal cost of producing the good by MC, Samuelson demonstrated that the optimal level of output in a community of n persons will satisfy the condition

$$\sum_{i=1}^{n} V_i = MC. \tag{2.1}$$

The satisfaction of equation 2.1 produces Samuelson equilibrium. As described in the Samuelson articles, equation 2.1 represents only the conditions for optimality in the production of public goods and not a true equilibrium in the sense that there is an equilibrating force moving the economy toward the satisfaction of that condition.[5] Samuelson suggested the difficulties that would be involved in designing a set of institutions which would produce optimality in public goods.[6]

Although the Samuelsonian optimality conditions were first formally developed to apply to Samuelson's polar definition of a public good, the conditions also described optimality under any conditions when all consumers must consume the same amount of a good.[7] If the good were purely private by Samuelson's definition, but with the restriction that $X_i = X/n$ for all i, then X amount of the good would have to be produced in order for individual i to receive X_i. Using again V_i to represent individual i's marginal valuation of the total amount of the good that is produced, equation 2.1 describes the optimality conditions, even though $\sum_{i=1}^{n} X_i = X$, meaning that the good is a Samuelsonian private good.

The Samuelsonian optimality condition is even more general than the above example and applies any time the amount of the good produced for one consumer implies a unique amount provided for all other consumers. In other words, a given level of total production of the good implies a unique level of consumption for each individual, so that

$$X_i = f_i(X). \tag{2.2}$$

Since X_i is a function of X and V_i is a function of X_i, then $V_i = g_i(X_i)$, so $V_i = g_i(f_i(X))$, or $V_i = h_i(X)$. Since the individual's marginal valuation of his consumption is a function of the total amount produced, the optimality condition is the condition stated in equation 2.1. This is true any time the restriction in equation 2.2 is present, and the original application to Samuelsonian public goods is merely a special case where $f_i(X) = X$ for all i at all levels of output. The optimality conditions would remain unchanged if X were a Samuelsonian private good, and

$$\sum_{i=1}^{n} f_i(X) = X.$$

This means that the Samuelsonian optimality conditions are fully applicable to any situation in which the institutional structure (or any other constraint) implies that the proportion of the total output of a good consumed by each consumer is uniquely implied by the level of output, so that equation 2.2 is satisfied. If a community is served by public schools, each family consumes that output in proportion to the number of children enrolled in the system. Given the public school system, the choice in the quantity dimension is whether to increase the output of the total system so that each individual can enjoy a proportional increase in output. This could be viewed as the choice that voters make when they decide in millage referenda whether to increase the school budget. Incidentally, a graphical analysis of the problem appears the same as in the Samuelsonian public goods case as well. The quantity axis simply measures some standard unit of output (for example, per pupil expenditures on education).

The Samuelsonian optimality conditions apply far more generally than was suggested in Samuelson's original articles. Whenever an individual is not excluded from consuming a homogeneous good, the units of a good can be defined in such a way that equation 2.2 is satisfied. For examples, per pupil educational expenditures, the number of lanes (or miles) on a highway, the national defense budget, the broadcast wattage of a television station, or the size of a municipal swimming pool could each be considered within this framework. The Samuelson equilibrium will be an optimum any time individuals cannot quantity-adjust independently of the group, and the good need not have any of the characteristics of Samuelsonian publicness. The unique characteristic that makes equation 2.2 imply the Samuelsonian optimality condition is that the total amount produced automatically implies the amount supplied to each consumer, and whether a good is Samuelsonian public or private or anywhere in between is irrelevant.

Bowen Equilibrium

The tendency for a majority rule system of government, under certain circumstances, to select the outcome most preferred by the median voter was first explicitly noted by Hotelling, and the idea was developed in detail by Howard Bowen.[8] The so-called median voter model, which produces Bowen equilibrium, is not a single model. Rather, there are several models that all produce the same result. The variants of the median voter model can be quickly sketched with the aid of Figure 2.1, where a community of five individuals has demand schedules D_1 through D_5, and the cost of production is divided evenly among them. Thus, each voter has a tax price equal to MC/5.

One variant of the model describes a committee process, in which one quantity of output, for example, Q_2, is proposed against another, Q_1, as motions in a majority rule election. The winning quantity Q_2 is then considered against another motion, such as Q^*. In this type of process, there is only one motion that can defeat every other motion: that motion is the one most preferred by the median voter.[9] The production of the outcome most

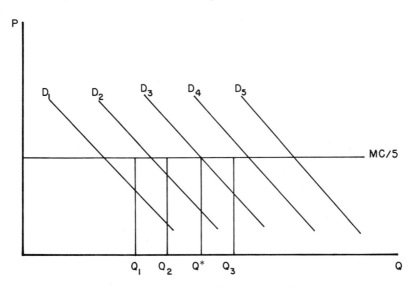

Fig. 2.1. The median voter model

preferred by the median voter is a Bowen equilibrium. In another variant of the model, voters vote for or against marginal increases of the good in a referendum process. A majority of the voters would approve of an increase in output from Q_2 to Q^*, but a referendum considering whether to increase output from Q^* to Q_3 would be defeated by a majority. This referendum process also results in Bowen equilibrium. In another variant of the model, voters elect representatives, and the elected representatives select the output to produce. The candidates select platforms containing a proposal for the output to be produced, and the winning candidate will tend toward Q^*. If one candidate selects Q_1 as his platform, the other can select Q_3, which is closer to the median, to win the votes of D_3, D_4, and D_5, and therefore win the election. The first candidate can defeat a platform of Q_3 with a platform of Q^*, and candidates will tend to converge upon the median. These various models lead to the general conclusion that a system of majority rule will result in Bowen equilibrium.

A closer look at these three main variants of the median voter model reveals that a number of assumptions must be fulfilled in each case for the models to work. In the committee process, each voter must have single peaked preferences or else there is the possibility that no motion will be able to defeat all others due to the well-known cycles described by Arrow.[10] In addition, there must be enough motions proposed that the median voter's most preferred outcome is among them. In the limit, this implies the possibility of an infinite number of motions. In the referendum model, additional increments to be voted on must be small enough to ensure that the median voter's preference is among the choices. Large increments could result in the agenda manipulation problem discussed in chapter 3. Also, voters must be assured that in the event of a failure, an additional referendum offering the marginal increase will be held. The political platform model relies on the assumptions that platforms can be ranked on a single-dimensioned continuum and that the platform of the candidate is the basis of the voter's choice. These assumptions will be analyzed more closely in the next chapter. Meanwhile, it is interesting to note that the empirical evidence on the subject overwhelmingly supports the conclusion of the median voter model.[11]

From an analytical standpoint, the median voter model is an extremely convenient way of aggregating public sector preferences. The median voter's demand curve can be used to represent revealed public sector preferences in the same way that a market demand curve aggregates the preferences of all consumers in a market. However, only under certain conditions will a Bowen equilibrium produce a Samuelson equilibrium.

Since the median voter will be in marginal equilibrium when his tax price, T_m, equals his marginal valuation, V_m, for the good, the Bowen equilibrium condition is[12]

$$V_m = T_m. \tag{2.3}$$

Since the cost of a good produced in the public sector is paid for by the taxes of the individuals in the society, $MC = \sum_{i=1}^{n} T_i$. Thus,

the Samuelsonian efficiency condition in equation 2.1 can be rewritten as

$$\sum_{i=1}^{n} V_i = \sum_{i=1}^{n} T_i. \tag{2.4}$$

In order for Bowen equilibrium to be efficient, equations 2.3 and 2.4 would have to be simultaneously satisfied, which implies[13]

$$V_m / \sum_{i=1}^{n} V_i = T_m / \sum_{i=1}^{n} T_i. \tag{2.5}$$

Equation 2.5 simply states that if the median voter's marginal tax share is the same proportion of the sum of the marginal tax shares as his marginal valuation is of the sum of the marginal valuations, then a Bowen equilibrium will simultaneously produce a Samuelson equilibrium. Although there may be good reason to suspect that the condition in equation 2.5 is not always fulfilled, the condition is substantially more general than the frequently employed assumption of symmetrically distributed demand curves.

Also worthy of note is the fact that Bowen equilibrium by itself makes no claim for economic efficiency. It is simply the result of an institutional process that is used for making social choices. This stands in contrast to the Samuelson equilibrium, which is economically efficient, although devoid of institutional content.[14]

Lindahl Equilibrium and Wicksellian Unanimity

The familiar concept of Lindahl equilibrium exists when each individual finds that his marginal tax price equals his marginal value for a good, or where

$$V_i = T_i, i = 1, n. \tag{2.6}$$

This conception of Lindahl equilibrium is in the spirit of Lindahl's analysis,[15] although Lindahl considered the mechanism of adjustment to be the altering of the percentage of the total cost paid by each individual. If an individual pays a lower percentage of the total cost, he will demand a larger quantity of output, and there will be one cost-sharing arrangement for which all individuals agree on the quantity of output to be produced. In Lindahl's framework, the individual considers his total tax bill—TC_i for individual i—and selects his most preferred level of output based upon the changes in TC_i for different levels of output. For the individual to be in equilibrium, $dTC_i/dX = V_i$ must be satisfied, and since $dTC_i/dX = T_i$, equation 2.6 is the Lindahl equilibrium condition.

There is a tendency to treat the T_i's as analogous to market prices, with the average price per unit also equal to T_i,[16] and to draw an analogy between Lindahl equilibrium in the public sector and competitive equilibrium in the private sector, since it appears that the same marginal conditions are satisfied. Under close examination, the analogy between the two concepts disappears. For one thing, in order to set every voter's marginal tax price equal to his average tax price at all possible levels of output, the marginal cost of the good must everywhere equal the average cost. Even with a constant marginal cost, though, there are more substantial weaknesses in the analogy.

Given the standard convexity assumptions, competitive market equilibrium prices are the only set of prices that will produce economic efficiency. The same is not true of Lindahl prices.

The optimal allocation of resources occurs in the public sector (when individual consumers cannot quantity-adjust) when the Samuelson equilibrium is produced, the Lindahl equilibrium is just one special case of Samuelson equilibrium. Any number of other cost-sharing arrangements could produce Samuelson equilibrium.

Lindahl prices do not necessarily result in what would be considered an equitable distribution of cost shares either. Denzau and Mackay have shown, for instance, that the individual who receives the greatest total benefit from a good could have the lowest Lindahl price.[17] In their example, an individual who lives next to the fire station could receive a high total value of protection, and thus the marginal value of additional protection would be low. The individual living far from the station receives little total protection, but has a high marginal value for additional protection, and thus has a high Lindahl price. While equity criteria would suggest that the individual living next to the fire station pay the most in taxes, Lindahl pricing would charge him the least.

Lindahl equilibrium does not necessarily produce an equitable distribution of cost shares and is not necessary for economic efficiency. The reason why each individual need not have his marginal tax price equal to his marginal valuation in order to produce efficiency is that the individual cannot quantity-adjust. He must accept the quantity of output which is produced for the whole group. Thus, for purposes of economic efficiency, as well as for equity, the individual's marginal tax price is irrelevant.

This can be illustrated in Figure 2.2, where the demands of three individuals are shown. All individuals could be charged the same tax price T2, and a majority rule political system that produced Bowen equilibrium would also produce Samuelson equilibrium. Lindahl pricing, charging D_1 price T3, D_2 price T2, and D_3 price T1, would be another cost-sharing arrangement that would produce Samuelson equilibrium under the same institutional setting. Another set of prices which would satisfy the Lindahl condition in equation 2.6 would be T1′, T2, T3′. In this case, the total tax paid by each individual would be the same as if all paid T2, even though T1′, T2, and T3′ satisfy equation 2.6, and so are Lindahl taxes. In both cases, the same output would be produced, and each taxpayer would pay the same amount, so every individual would find no difference between Lindahl tax shares T1', T2, and T3', and an equal division of taxes. The point is that when individuals cannot marginally adjust, their marginal tax prices are irrelevant.

On purely economic grounds, Lindahl pricing has nothing in particular to recommend it. Other tax schemes could be just as efficient and may be more equitable. The reason is that the individual cannot choose the quantity that he will consume. Still, Lindahl prices have an important characteristic: all individuals are in agreement as to how much of the good should be produced.

Despite the fact that with output Q_2 in Figure 2.2 individuals would be indifferent between Lindahl prices T1', T2, T3', and

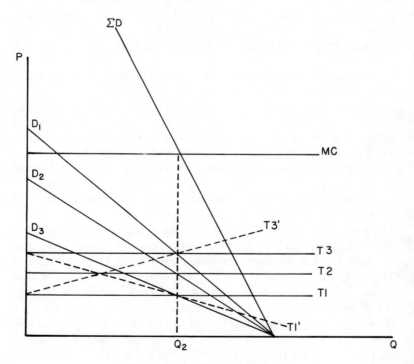

Fig. 2.2. Lindahl equilibrium

identical tax prices where all pay T2, with the identical tax prices, individual 1 will want more output while individual 3 will want less. With any tax sharing arrangement, individuals would always prefer lower taxes; but Lindahl pricing is the only taxation method that produces a unanimous agreement on the amount of output to be produced. The characteristic of unanimous agreement on the amount of output, given tax shares, will by itself produce a Samuelson equilibrium.

The significance of Lindahl equilibrium may be as much political as economic. If Lindahl tax shares can be designed, then all individuals will be in agreement as to the amount of output to be produced, which makes it more likely that production will take place efficiently. If, in Figure 2.2, all indviduals have tax price T2, individual 3 would prefer substantially less than Q_2. If he is politically powerful, he may be able to work through the political system to reduce the amount of output below the efficient level.

Viewed in this context, there is a great deal of similarity between the concepts of Lindahl equilibrium and Wicksellian unanimity.[18] Wicksell suggested that if a public expenditure was cost effective, then tax shares could be set in such a manner that there would be a unanimous agreement in favor of the expenditure. Wicksell then recommended that voters consider various financing proposals, along with proposals for public expenditures, and that a unanimous agreement be required for the expenditures to be undertaken.[19] Lindahl prices are the tax shares that would be needed to produce Wicksellian unanimity. In a political setting characterized by Lindahl equilibrium/Wicksellian unanimity, efficient decisions would be more likely to be made, and a majority of individuals would have less power to exploit a minority.[20]

In summary, Lindahl equilibrium is a special case of Samuelson equilibrium, since if $V_i = T_i$ for all i, then $\sum V_i = \sum T_i$. It is also a special case of Bowen equilibrium, since $V_m = T_m$. But while Lindahl equilibrium does provide an efficient allocation of resources, it is not unique in this respect. Lindahl equilibrium also has no special equity properties to recommend it. The special characteristic of Lindahl equilibrium is that it produces a unanimous agreement with respect to the amount of output to be produced.

Tiebout Equilibrium

The Tiebout model is a model of local government activity and has as its mechanism of adjustment the movement of individuals from less preferred to more preferred political jurisdictions.[21] City managers, according to Tiebout, perform the entrepreneurial function of tailoring city output to the demands of the residents, with each resident being free to move to the locality that best satisfies his demands. Tiebout's article describes the general mechanism of adjustment to optimality,[22] and the adjustment process can be considered within the same general framework as has been used for the other concepts of public sector equilibrium in this chapter.

Consider the community of three individuals shown in Figure 2.3, which is much like the community in Figure 2.2. The marginal cost of producing the local government output is MC, and all individuals must agree on an amount to be produced. The Samuelson equilibrium level of output is Q_2, which is also Bowen equilibrium because of the construction of Figure 2.3.

The adjustment mechanism toward optimality in the Tiebout model is initiated by the ability of the residents of a community to move to another of the large number of possible communities. For the purpose of this chapter, three communities will be a sufficiently large number, and all communities will be assumed to have individuals identical to those in the community represented by Figure 2.3. Without mobility among the communities, the most efficient level of output in each community would be Samuelson equilibrium quantity Q_2. As was earlier mentioned, the original Samuelson articles described no adjustment process that lead toward optimality, and Tiebout's article was written in part as a response to Samuelson, showing that an adjustment process could exist if individuals could move from one governmental jurisdiction to another.[23]

With three communities like those in Figure 2.3, Tiebout equilibrium allocates resources more efficiently than producing Q_2 in each community. City managers, having the incentive of providing the allocation of resources most desirable to the residents, would produce Q_1 in one city, Q_2 in another city, and Q_3 in the third city. This would entice the three individuals with

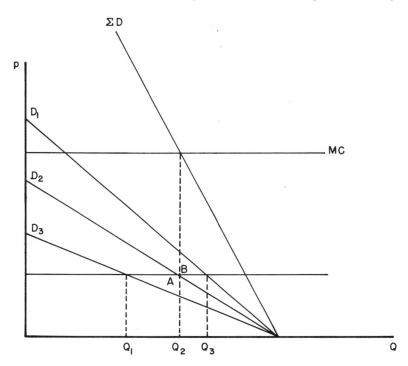

Fig. 2.3. Tiebout equilibrium

demands like D_3 to live in the first city, with the D_2's in the second and the D_1's in the third city. The resulting efficiency gain would be three times the areas of triangles A and B, which would provide some surplus that could be divided in such a way to provide an entrepreneurial incentive.

The Tiebout equilibrium allows adjustment in another dimension not available in the earlier discussed equilibrium concepts, but several notable characteristics exist in Tiebout equilibrium. For one thing, every individual is charged a Lindahl price in equilibrium. Also, the per unit prices charged to each individual will tend to be the same across individuals. In order to charge different per unit prices to different individuals, some individuals will be charged an above average price. In a model of intergovernmental competition, those individuals would be valuable residents, and communities would try to bid for them by offering slightly lower prices. The competitive process would end only when uniform per unit prices were charged. The competitive process would also result in efficiency gains as different communities offer different levels of output to entice potential residents.

While some of the fine points of the theoretical model may have limitations, the basic model suggests strong efficiency reasons for intergovernmental competition on two grounds. First, the problem of demand revelation for public goods is better over come than without intergovermental competition. Second, a Tiebout equilibrium will tend to be more efficient with mobility than a Samuelson equilibrium when there is not a mechanism to group similar consumers together. A third reason might also be mentioned: If political agreement is important, as was noted in the previous section, then there will be more of a consensus of opinion in Tiebout equilibrium than in a general Lindahl equilibrium in which tax shares will be more open to debate. In Tiebout equilibrium, competitive forces will tend to equalize tax prices. In this respect, Tiebout equilibrium is a special case of Lindahl equilibrium. Individuals with similar demands are grouped together, so that the Lindahl condition $T_i = V_i$ for all i is satisfied, and the adjustment process produces $T_i = T_j$ for all i and j.

In closing this section, it might be worthwhile to note that while Tiebout developed his model for individuals who move from one community to another, the model applies more generally to any type of intergovernmental competition.[24] Thus, on these grounds alone, a voucher system of education[25] would be more efficient than a single school system, and a gain in efficiency sould result from allowing individuals to choose their pension system, rather than being forced to take Social Security. This would be true even if the uniform system produced Samuelson equilibrium for the population as a whole.

Niskanen Equilibrium

The final concept of public sector equilibrium to be discussed, Niskanen equilibrium, is mentioned not because of the significance of the specific nature of the equilibrium, nor because there might be some situation in the real world which resembles Niskanen equilibrium.[26] Rather, it will be analyzed because it is the most rigorous attempt at conceptualizing the institutional structure of public sector supply. This factor alone makes the concept a significant step in the development of an economic theory of the public sector.[27] The earlier concepts discussed in this chapter have been primarily concerned with the aggregation of individual demands for public sector output. Calling those concepts equilibria has tacitly assumed that the government produces the output determined through the demand aggregation process.

By contrast, Niskanen assumes that government output is produced by self-interested bureaucrats in the same way that micro theory assumes self-interest. Such an assumption seems very appropriate to the economics literature, since the standard justification for government activity is that self-interested behavior sometimes leads to market failure. If individuals in the market act in their own self-interest when it is against the best interest of society as a whole, there is no reason to believe that they would behave differently just because they are employed by the government. Stated more bluntly, without the assumption of self-interested behavior, the economic rationale for governmental activity disappears. Since bureaucrats cannot (legally) keep profits, Niskanen suggests that they are after other things, such as a high salary, power, prestige, ease of running the bureau, and so forth. All of these things are furthered by increases in the bureau's budget; thus, Niskanen assumes that bureaucrats are budget maximizers.

The budget maximizing bureaucrats do not make marginal sales, as do market enterprisers. Instead, each year they exchange a total budget for a total output, which makes the resulting equilibrium an outcome of a bargaining process. The bureau's superior knowledge and expertise allows it to place the purchaser of the output on the all-or-nothing demand curve, so that Q units of output of the good X will be produced, where

$$\int_{Q=0}^{x} T_m = \int_{Q=0}^{x} V_m. \qquad (2.7)$$

Implied in this representation of Niskanen equilibrium is that demand for public sector output is aggregated through the median voter model. This Niskanen equilibrium is a kind of median voter model, but instead of satisfying equation 2.3, the equilibrium condition in equation 2.7 implies

$$T_m > V_m \tag{2.8}$$

in Niskanen equilibrium.[28] In other words, the median voter's marginal tax price is greater than his marginal valuation of public sector output.

While this is an interesting theoretical finding, perhaps a bigger contribution of this work is the development of a rigorous model of public sector supply. Niskanen equilibrium differs from the other concepts discussed in that the individuals who produce public sector output are considered as utility-maximizing counterparts to entrepreneurs in the private sector.[29] Since its appearance, Niskanen's book has stimulated a large amount of research on bureaucratic institutions, which has helped the theory of public sector supply to advance toward the level of the literature on public sector demand.[30]

Conclusion

The purpose of this chapter has been to describe and relate some of the more common concepts of public sector equilibrium. By analyzing the concepts in their simplest forms, and all within the same basic framework, we hope the most important similarities and differences among the concepts have been emphasized. Some of the concepts, such as Samuelson equilibrium and Lindahl equilibrium, describe optimality conditions rather than equilibrating mechanisms.[31] Others, such as Bowen equilibrium and Niskanen equilibrium are models of institutional processes which make no claims for optimality. Wicksellian unanimity and Tiebout equilibrium are models of institutional processes which produce efficient outcomes. The distinction between models that describe optimality conditions and models that describe institutional processes leading to equilibrium is fundamental to understanding the concepts.

Although these concepts are frequently applied to Samuelsonian public goods, the Samuelsonian definition of a public good is not central to any one of the concepts. The characteristic that makes Samuelsonian equilibrium efficient is that each individual's consumption of the good is a function of the total amount produced, and a Samuelsonian public good is only one instance where this characteristic may be present. Also worthy of note is the fact that Lindahl equilibrium has no special claim as the public sector analog to competitive equilibrium in the private sector. When the consumption of one individual implies the consumption levels of all other individuals, prices for everyone except the decision-makers are irrelevant to economic efficiency. The advantage of Lindahl equilibrium is more political than economic in that it implies unanimous agreement with respect to the amount of the good to be produced.

These concepts are at the foundation of much of the literature in public sector economics, and also provide the basis for upcoming chapters. The next chapter, about agenda control, is based upon the referendum model of Bowen equilibrium presented by Bowen in his original article. The conclusions of the relatively new agenda control literature are similar to those that Niskanen developed, but the models are based upon the same concepts as the Bowen model. Chapter 4 considers the median voter model in light of the agenda control literature, and finds that in the cases that have been empirically tested, referenda seem to yield Bowen equilibrium. Chapters 5 and 6 are also built explicitly on the Bowen model. Chapter 5 presents a referendum system once used in Florida that guarantees a Bowen equilibrium outcome. Chapter 6 demonstrates that the Bowen equilibrium level of output can be increased when politicans can vary tax shares as a part of their political platforms. With that preview, chapter 3 will analyze Bowen equilibrium and the median voter model more carefully within the agenda control framework.

Agenda Control in the Median Voter Model

Imagine that an individual is about to vote in an election that will select the president of a group, and the president is to be elected by majority rule. The group might be a club, a professional association, or a nation. The voter examines the ballot, and discovers that only one candidate is listed for the office of president. While the voter may have many alternatives, from refusing to vote to writing in another individual's name, in this situation the single candidate listed on the ballot will be overwhelmingly likely to win the election.

From this simple example it is obvious that if a nominating committee has the power to determine what alternatives are to be placed on the ballot, that committee has a tremendous ability to control the outcome of an election. Even though the winner would receive a majority of the votes, the nominating committee clearly can manipulate the agenda in a way that could keep the outcome from being truly representative of the preferences of a majority of the voters. Controlling the agenda by placing a single candidate on the ballot is not uncommon. Organizations as diverse as communist governments and the Southern Economic Association present their voters with a ballot containing only one candidate for president.

While offering only one candidate on the ballot is the most extreme and obvious case of agenda control, the agenda setter will still have the potential to manipulate the outcome of an election when more than one choice is offered. Another obvious example would be running the nominating committee's choice for office against a clearly unacceptable candidate. Unless the voters are willing to protest by electing an otherwise unacceptable candidate, they are forced to accept the nominating committee's choice—even though there may be an obvious third candidate who could easily defeat the other two if only the individual could be placed on the ballot. Romer and Rosenthal have called the individual or group that selects the options to be placed before the voters the agenda setter,[1] and the purpose of this chapter is to discuss the potential of the agenda setter for controlling the outcome of an election.

The agenda control literature has been developed within the framework of the median voter model, so this chapter will begin with a deeper look at the median voter model than the discussion of chapter 2. The model of agenda control will then be developed within the same framework, followed by a discussion of the applicability and implications of the potential for agenda control.

The Median Voter Model

One of the most significant developments in the public choice literature is the median voter model. The median voter model describes a process of taxpayer choice through the institution of voting which parallels the economic theory of consumer choice through the institution of the market and, in so doing, provides a theoretical link between taxation and expenditures. The importance of this theoretical link is demonstrated by the fact that the median voter model is so frequently employed in both the theoretical and the empirical work in public choice and public finance.

The term "median voter model" generally refers not to a single model, but to a single conclusion that follows from any one of several models. The models all begin from a common starting point. A single political issue is to be determined by a simple majority voting rule, via some election process. The alternatives may all be ranked along a single-dimensioned continuum, and all voters have single-peaked preferences.[2] Several different models of the election process may be used to arrive at the conclusion that the alternative most preferred by the median voter will be the alternative selected by majority rule.

The three basic models, sketched in chapter 2, are the committee model, the referendum model, and the representative democracy model. The infant agenda control literature has been developed mainly within the referendum model, which will be developed at length in this chapter. But the implications of the agenda control model are probably just as significant in the other two types of models, as the example at the beginning of the chapter suggests. The literature to date has barely scratched the surface, since some of the more interesting questions concern an integration of the agenda control model with theories of political parties and special interest groups to see how they might influence party platforms and the platforms of candidates on the ballot. Discussion of these issues will be deferred, however, in order to examine the concept of agenda control in a referendum.

Voter Behavior in Referenda

Before the results of referenda can be used to evaluate the preferences of voters, a theory of voter behavior must be developed in order to interpret the results of referenda. The utility function of a voter can be represented as

$$U = U(Q, G_1, G_2, \ldots, G_n), \tag{3.1}$$

where U represents the individual's level of utility, Q is the quantity of the good to be voted on in a referendum, and G_1 through G_n are all of the other goods the individual consumes. The theory in this chapter will not consider price changes for any goods except Q, so equation 3.1 can be rewritten as

$$U = V(Q, G) \tag{3.2}$$

by invoking Hicks's composite goods theorem,[3] where G is all other goods. The individual will face a budget constraint of the form $Y = P_eQ + P_GG$, where Y is the individual's nominal income, and P_e and P_G are the nominal prices of Q and other goods. Holding the nominal price of other goods constant, $G = Y/K - (P_eQ)/K$, which can be substituted for G in equation 3.2 to yield

$$U = W(Y, Q, P_e); \overline{P}_1, \overline{P}_2, \ldots, \overline{P}_n. \tag{3.3}$$

Equation 3.3 states that, holding the prices of all other goods constant, the individual's well-being is a function of his nominal income and the price and quantity of Q that he receives.

Assuming that W exhibits the standard convexity properties, and holding Y constant, U can be graphed into the P_e-Q plane by varying Q and P_e and tracing the contours for which these changes leave the voter indifferent. Figure 3.1 illustrates this experiment in a two-good case. In panel B, the vertical axis measures the amount of all other goods. When his budget constraint is AC, his most preferred quantity of Q is Q*. Holding his nominal income and the price of all other goods constant, P_e can be lowered so that his budget constraint becomes AC'. In order for the voter to remain indifferent to the price change, he would have to consume either Q' or Q'' at the new price. Panel A depicts this same experiment in the P_e-Q plane, where the original price is C and the new price is C'. Q', Q*, and Q'' are the same as in panel B. The experiment demonstrates the three points (C', Q'), (C, Q*), and (C', Q'') to be on the same indifference curve. For simplicity, a constant marginal cost is assumed by measuring the quantity of the good in terms of the number of dollars spent per capita on the good. By measuring the quantity of the good in this way, everybody within a governmental unit must consume the same quantity.

Curves U1, U2, U3, and U4 are four of the voter's indifference curves, graphed in the P_e-Q plane. Since a lower price per unit increases the individual's utility, and a larger quantity is also a good in his utility function, the individual prefers points at the lower right of the graph; thus, U4 is preferred to U3, which is preferred to U2, and so forth. The slopes of the curves show diminishing marginal rates of substitution between a lower price and a larger quantity.

If the price per unit is fixed at C, the individual's most preferred quantity is Q*. Thus, point E is one point on the individual's demand curve. At point E, horizontal line CMC is tangent to U4, meaning that the first derivative of U4 at E is zero. The demand curve, FG, is the locus of all points at which an indifference curve has a first derivative of zero. AB is the individual's marginal valuation curve, given cost curve CMC. It lies above FG to the left of E and below FG to the right of E because of its absence of income effects.[4]

Modeling the Referendum Process

Using the preference function just developed to describe the median voter, the voter's interpretation of the referendum process

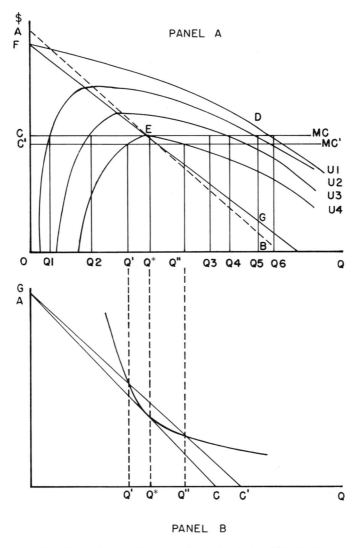

Fig. 3.1. The median voter's choice in a referendum

can be modeled. In developing a framework for the model, the emphasis will be on the demand side of the public sector. Accordingly, many of the problems associated with efficiently supplying goods in the public sector will be disregarded. For example, this section will assume that the production of public sector output is process efficient,[5] and that voters receive the output that they vote for. Some theoretical sources of efficiency will also be excluded from this model. The model will specify that the agenda setter is separate from the voters; and that side payments or vote trading do not occur among the voters.[6] At the outset, the model will concentrate specifically on the information transferred through referenda. In this model, the agenda setter formulates a proposal to provide public sector output to a group of voters who must pay the entire cost of the output. The proposal includes both the quantity of the good to be provided and the tax that each individual must pay if the proposal is passed. Tax shares will be considered given and invariant, in order to preclude the possibility that the agenda setter will propose to tax a minority in order to provide the good to the majority. The agenda setter will be able to propose tax rates but will have no power to change the proportion of the total tax paid by each voter.[7] Proposals will be accepted or rejected by majority rule.

The voter's interpretation of the referendum process will lie somewhere on a continuum between two polar extremes. On the one end, the voter may view the referendum process as strictly limited to the two alternatives in the referendum. The referendum gives the voter the opportunity to vote for additional spending, which will increase the public sector output, or the voter can vote against paying taxes and have a lower level of output. In this conception, the referendum is a two-point offer, since the voter's only alternatives are to vote either for or against all additional spending. This conception of the referendum process can be illustrated with the use of Figure 3.1.

First examine the case where none of the good is initially being provided, so that the voter is put in an all-or-nothing situation. The electorate can either accept all of the output the agenda setter proposes to provide, or reject the issue and have none. The median voter will, therefore, approve of any proposal that puts him on a higher indifference curve than no output of the good. In this case, any proposal between 0 and Q6 will be accepted. Note that U1 is the locus of points for which, when average cost equals the ordinate of U1, the individual is indifferent between consuming the quantity on the curve or none of the good. That is, U1 is the individual's all-or-nothing demand curve.

The voter deciding to accept or reject any proposal will approve of any plan that will yield positive net benefits. Thus, in the example where no education is currently being provided, any proposal between 0 and Q5 will be approved by a majority. If some of the good is already being provided, the set of proposals that will be approved by a majority will diminish in size. For example, if Q1 is currently being provided, and the agenda setter formulates a proposal to produce additional output, only those proposals between Q1 and Q4 will be approved by a majority. The closer the existing quantity is to the Bowen equilibrium quantity, the smaller the range of proposals around Bowen equilibrium which would be approved by a majority of the voters becomes. Thus, in cases where the existing quantity is already close to the Bowen equilibrium quantity, single elections will approximate marginal adjustments. Still, voters perceive the single election as a two-point offer instead of an opportunity to make marginal adjustments.

This two-point offer model of the referendum process is the foundation of the public choice literature on agenda control. The agenda setter has the power to offer an alternative to the status quo, and only the agenda setter's single alternative appears on the ballot to oppose the status quo. If the status quo is below the median voter's most preferred level of output, then the agenda setter has the power to increase output beyond the median voter's most preferred level via the presentation of a two-point offer that would leave the median voter almost indifferent between the status quo and the higher level of expenditures. This view of the referendum process differs significantly from the standard median voter model described in the last chapter.

The standard conception of the referendum process pictures the voter believing that if the present referendum fails, a new referendum will be held offering a level of output marginally lower than the previously defeated rate. Referenda would continue to be held until a level of output was approved. Voters do not associate any transactions costs with the election process, so they are willing to continue returning to the polls until the process is completed. The election process is illustrated in Figure 3.1, where the preferences illustrated are those of the median voter.

Initially, quantity Q1 is provided, and the agenda setter formulates a proposal to increase output to Q3. The median voter will not approve this proposal, even if Q3 is preferred to Q1, because the voter knows that should the election fail, a slightly smaller amount will be proposed which will be preferred to either Q1 or Q3. After Q3 fails, Q″ will be proposed, and will fail for the same reason. The agenda setter then proposes Q*, which is approved by the median voter, and all voters that prefer a larger quantity than Q*. Those preferring a smaller quantity will vote against the proposal, hoping that a still smaller proposal will be forwarded by the agenda setter. Thus, Q* will be provided, and will be approved by a bare majority of the voters.

This second model conforms with the referendum variant of the median voter model described in the last chapter, and demonstrates that referenda can lead to Bowen equilibrium under a strict set of assumptions. The initial proposal must be larger than Bowen equilibrium; and the voter must be assured that in the event of a failure, a new election will be held offering a marginally lower level of output. If the increment of change from one election to the next is too large, then the voter will view the election as a two-point offer. When transactions costs are included in the analysis, the voter could again be inclined to view the election as a two-point offer instead of a step in a marginal adjustment process.

The Power to Control the Agenda

Seeing how the basic model of agenda control operates, two questions come to mind. First, why would the agenda setter want to produce more than the median voter's preference, and, second, how does the institutional framework allow the agenda setter to control the outcome of a majority rule election? The question concerning the motives of the agenda setter will be deferred until later in the chapter. Assuming that the agenda setter does want a larger output than the median voter, how can the larger output be approved by a majority of the voters?

The first thing to note is that the utility functions and behavior of voters are the same within the agenda control model as they are within the median voter model as described by Bowen, Downs, and its other developers. The difference is only in the proposals that the voters may consider. The median voter model was developed in three variants in the last chapter. For purposes of analysis, a brief discussion of the applicability of agenda control to each variant will be worthwhile. Since the agenda control model has been developed within the context of a referendum model, the committee model and the representative government model will be examined first.

Within the committee model, members of a committee are free to bring forward motions on how much of a good should be produced. Given the assumptions common to both the standard median voter model and the agenda control model, when no limits are placed on the number of proposals, the median voter's most preferred proposal is the only motion that can defeat all other proposals in a majority rule vote. The key distinction between this model and the agenda control model is that the voters are the group that can set the agenda. When the voters and the agenda setter are the same group, a Bowen equilibrium results. Within this setting, what if there were a limit to the number of motions that could be put forward? There could be a constitutional limit on the number of motions, or a time constraint, or some other reason why motions were costly to bring to the floor. Under this type of institutional arrangement, a very common type of constraint is that motions to be considered at a meeting must be submitted to the chair some specified time period before the meeting. The median voter might not submit a motion under any of these cases, and the median voter's motion could not win if it were not nominated.

Under these circumstances, the median voter's motion might not be selected, but there would be no bias toward either larger or smaller levels of output as long as all members of the committee have equal access to the agenda. Transactions costs within the committee model might imply that actual outcomes will not always be the median voter's most preferred outcome, but equal access to the agenda by the voters should imply that the average outcome is the median voter's preference. Equal access to the agenda should yield an unbiased distribution of election results about the median, rather than the biased results predicted in the agenda control model.

Concern about equal access to the agenda is important, since equal access alone should produce unbiased results around the median, if not the Bowen equilibrium itself. Would this conclusion extend to representative government as well, if representatives are chosen by an unbiased process? The answer is a qualified yes. As long as individuals' preferences are not affected by being elected as representatives, then an unbiased selection of representatives should lead to a Bowen equilibrium. There is the possibility that, once elected, representatives would desire larger levels of outputs. The incentives of representatives will be discussed later, but this discussion does serve to draw the line between the committee model and a model of representative government. The committee model can be expected to lead to a Bowen equilibrium, but the key assumption is that all voters have equal access to the agenda.

In the Downsian model of representative government, voters elect representatives who determine the output to be produced for the group. Candidates present platforms to the voters, and in Downs's model voters choose their representatives based upon the candidates' platforms. Bowen equilibrium results. The assumptions about the issue space and the preferences and behavior of voters are the same in this model as in the agenda control model. The only difference is in the way that issues are presented to the voters. In the Downsian representative democracy model, candidates may choose any platform they desire, but only the median voter's most preferred platform can defeat any other platform. Realizing this, both candidates have an incentive to move toward the center of the political spectrum to present the median platform to voters.

A casual examination reveals that the simple Downsian model explains many features of the political system of the United States. Voters frequently complain that they are not given a true choice in elections, since candidates all seem so much alike. The theory predicts this by saying that both candidates should be trying to appeal to the median—or, in Richard Nixon's terminology, the silent majority. The theory also predicts that extreme candidates cannot win elections, which is supported by the presidential campaigns of Barry Goldwater and George Mc-Govern. The theory even explains why a winner-take-all democracy should be characterized by only two political parties. With both candidates aiming for the median voter, a third party would have to erode either one party's support or the other's, since the new party would be likely to arise either well to the left or well to the right of the median. (The median voter, after all, already has two parties trying to support that platform. Demand for a new party would be from voters not close to the median.) The result is that only one viable party remains, and in order to win any elections, the two remaining parties must merge, or one must go out of business.[8] The point is that the real world operation of political competition seems to support this version of the median voter model.

As a model of the election process, this model assumes that candidates are elected based only on their platforms, and that voters are able to identify candidates' stands on issues. As a model of public sector output, the model also assumes that the platforms of the campaigning candidates describe their actual behavior once elected. If candidates must be periodically reelected, then they do have some incentive to perform as promised.

The median voter model has been used as the foundation of much of the public choice literature, and the decision to produce most public sector output is made through elected representatives rather than through a committee or referendum process. Therefore, this representative government model is the basis for most of the theoretical and empirical conclusions based on the median voter model. In the agenda control model of the referendum process, most agenda setters will be elected representatives. In this case, simply explaining why the agenda setter has the incentive and the power to manipulate the agenda in order to increase public sector output beyond the level most preferred by the median voter does not address the complete issue. Why can a competing agenda setter not run for office under the median voter's most preferred platform and defeat the incumbent? Almost all public sector output is proposed by elected representatives, and only a small portion must then be approved by referendum. If the agenda control model accurately describes the referendum process, then it is a sign of a much more general problem, since a referendum can never enhance the ability of governments to increase output, but can (and does in the agenda control model) act as a constraint. This is not meant to pass judgment on the agenda control model, but simply to note that if it is an accurate description of reality, then the real problem lies with representative government.

The Incentives of the Agenda Setter

Once the agenda setter is in a position to control the agenda, the assumptions behind the agenda control model appear reasonable, as do the assumptions of the Bowen model of the referendum process. The difference between the two is the motive behind the agenda setter. Under most circumstances, the agenda setter who desires to manipulate the outcome of a referendum will have at least some power to do so. But for the agenda setter who desires a Bowen equilibrium, a referendum will provide additional information to assist. It should again be noted that the agenda setter trying to enlarge the budget would never prefer a referendum over the ability to set the budget level without a referendum, since the referendum can only act as a constraint.

There are a number of reasons why the agenda setter should want to propose the Bowen equilibrium level of output in a referendum. If the agenda setter were elected in a majority rule setting, then the representative government model would predict that the agenda setter would have been elected under the median voter's most preferred platform. Elected agenda setters are likely to have platforms coincidental with the median voter's preference. The most compelling reason to believe that the agenda setter would want to propose the median voter's preference is that this is the action that would be most likely to result in the reelection of the agenda setter. Reelection, or election to a higher office based on the candidate's past record, must be important to a politician.

On the other side of the argument, agenda setters may respond more to special interest groups than to voters in general. This would be especially true if voters in general are relatively uninformed about issues. An extension of this argument would imply that single issue agenda setters would face closer voter scrutiny than multiple issue setters, since voters would be more able to judge their satisfaction on one issue than on many. School boards should therefore be less able to manipulate agendas than state legislators. Another factor that could foster increased budgets through agenda control is that individuals favorably disposed to an activity would have more of an incentive to become the agenda setters. High demanders of education, for example, would be more likely to run for a position on the school board. In addition, agenda setters may find their jobs more agreeable if they favor larger budgets. To use the example of schools again, school boards will have more interaction with educational administrators than voters. This interaction with a high demand special interest group would be more agreeable the more closely the objectives of the agenda setter coincided with the budgeted governmental entity it was overseeing.

There appear to be good arguments on both sides of the agenda control issue, and the particular details of the institutional structure of individual cases may ultimately determine which model best describes the referendum process. Under some circumstances, agenda manipulation may result in larger outlays than the median voter would prefer, while in other cases referenda may lead to Bowen equilibrium. Some empirical issues are discussed in the next chapter.

The Niskanen Model

There may be a tendency to draw too close a parallel between the agenda control model of referenda and the Niskanen model of bureaucracy. The similarity is that both have the potential in the extreme case to place the median voter in an all-or-nothing equilibrium. The process by which this equilibrium is reached is totally different, however. In Niskanen's model, the bureau is in a superior bargaining position because of its superior knowledge of the output it supplies. The bureau has no power to control the agenda, at least in the sense in which the term "agenda control" is used with reference to referenda. The bureau's sponsor is free to ask for any level of output, but the bureau has as incentive to disguise its true cost functions in order to lead the sponsor to believe that the all-or-nothing equilibrium is the best level of output the sponsor could receive.[9] The bureau is able to misrepresent its cost conditions to the sponsor because the bureau is the ultimate source of that information. The bureau is staffed by the experts on its output and works full-time in producing the output. The sponsor, by contrast, probably oversees many bureaus, probably has fewer members than the bureau, and in any event will have to get cost data from the bureau. From the theorist's seat of omniscience, the sponsor appears to be in an all-or-nothing equilibrium; but with the limited information that the sponsor possesses the Niskanen equilibrium appears to be the best alternative for the sponsor. If the sponsor is representative of the median voter, then the Niskanen equilibrium will also be a Bowen equilibrium, because given the information available to the voter, the output produced is the output the median voter would most prefer.

The agenda control model is completely different in this respect. The median voter knows that the output produced is larger than Bowen equilibrium, and the median voter would immediately change that output if it were possible. While both the agenda control equilibrium and the Niskanen equilibrium resemble all-or-nothing sales, there is an important distinction. In the Niskanen equilibrium, the sponsor is free to choose any level of output, but chooses the Niskanen equilibrium level due to the biased information received from the bureau. With agenda manipulation, the median voter knows that his most preferred level of output is not offered by the agenda setter.

Other Models of Agenda Control

The referendum model of agenda control developed in this chapter originally appeared in the later half of the 1970s,[10] but many other writers both before and after have modeled a process of governmental decision making that produces outcomes exploiting the monopoly power of government.[11] For example, Buchanan and Flowers speculated in 1969 that a Taxpayers' Revolution was due to the actual level of expenditures being significantly in excess of Bowen equilibrium.[12] The equilibrium described by Buchanan and Flowers is the same as in the agenda control model, and so foreshadowed the development of that model. However, the basic concept of agenda control predates this literature, and discusses control of the mix of expenditures rather than the level.

Buchanan noted that the alteration of the mix of government output will affect the total budget that the voters would most prefer.[13] Within the model in this chapter, the relevant part of Buchanan's argument is that the median voter's most preferred budget will increase as the share of the government budget commanded by goods with more elastic demands increases. Some mix of government expenditures will be optimal, and within the Bowen model the median voter's most preferred mix would lead to a Bowen equilibrium with a certain budget size. By increasing the share of the budget devoted to goods with relatively elastic demands, the Bowen equilibrium budget level would increase. Thus, the agenda setter would have the power to increase the Bowen equilibrium level of expenditures by adjusting the mix of public sector output.

Plott and Levine have made a similar argument, noting that the agenda setter can affect the outcome of a voting process if the setter can determine the order in which alternatives are to be considered.[14] Within a three-alternative example of a cyclical majority, the effect of the order would be obvious: the last proposal made would win.

These models of agenda control all have as their common element that the median voter's choice set is restricted in some dimension by the agenda setter for the purpose of manipulating the outcome of the election. The agenda setter can limit the quantity alternatives that the voter has so that the median voter's most preferred quantity is not in the choice set, or he can alter the mix of output from the most preferred by the median voter, or present the alternatives in such an order that the setter's most preferred outcome wins the majority approval. These methods of agenda control all have as a common element that the median voter would prefer a different agenda setter who, as in the Downs model, would offer the median voter's most preferred platform.

Agenda control in this sense, then, means that the agenda setter presents an agenda that does not contain the median voter's most preferred outcome in order to manipulate the outcome of the election.[15] Within a larger setting, a Downsian model of representative democracy that selects agenda setters would tend to select against this type of outcome, and agenda setters facing reelection would have incentives not to engage in this type of agenda control. In short, the median voter will find the agenda setter antagonistic, and will have an incentive to eliminate the agenda setter or at least alter the setter's behavior. Within these agenda control models, the agenda setter acts against the best interest of the median voter.

Control of Benefit Shares and Tax Shares

Two other variables that the agenda setter might be able to control are benefit shares and tax shares. Chapter 6 explains in detail the implications of the manipulation of tax shares, and control of benefit shares yields the same results, so the discussion here will be brief.[16] In the case of taxation, the agenda setter can lower the median voter's tax share by raising everyone else's tax share. As a result the price per unit of government output to the median voter declines, and the median voter will demand a larger level of output.[17] With benefit shares, the median voter's benefit share would be increased by decreasing the benefit shares of the other voters, with the same result. The price per unit of government output declines, and the median voter demands more.[18] The result is an increased Bowen equilibrium budget. In either case, the increased Bowen equilibrium budget results from an increase of the benefit to tax share ratio of the median voter.

There is a crucial distinction between control of the median voter's benefit/tax ratio and agenda control as it has been discussed in the rest of this chapter, however. The earlier agenda control models all left the median voter worse off as a result of the manipulation of the agenda setter, whereas the increase in the median voter's benefit/tax ratio improves the well-being of the median voter. For this reason, the two types of models will generally be applicable to different types of circumstances.

In a situation where agenda setters are selected through a Downsian process of political competition, the candidate for agenda setter who proposes a platform of agenda control through two-point offers or manipulation of the expenditure mix would be defeated by the candidate who proposes a platform against such agenda control. For this reason, these types of agenda control models are appropriately labeled models of monopoly government. If the selection of agenda setters were competitive, this type of agenda setter would be unable to remain in office. By contrast, the candidate who offers an increased benefit/tax ratio to the median voter would have an advantage in the Downsian process of selecting the agenda setter. Indeed, competition for the position of agenda setter encourages the manipulation of benefit/tax ratios even though the other forms of agenda control are discouraged.

Manipulation of benefit/tax ratios is a feature of competitive government rather than monopoly government. A lower benefit/tax ratio for the median voter implies a higher rate for the high demanders, meaning that even though the government budget is larger, high demanders may be worse off as a result of higher tax shares. Very likely, the commonly stated incentives for the setter to increase the budget will disappear in this type of model, since the high demanders of government would ordinarily be considered as the proponents of a higher budget. Additional discussion will be deferred until chapter 6, but the important distinction between these types of models must be emphasized here.

Both types of models lead to increased government budgets. The monopoly government models do so while making the median voter worse off, so these models are inconsistent with political competition in the Downsian sense. By contrast, the competitive government models that alter benefit/tax ratios are a part of the Downsian political competition, and candidates have an incentive to alter their platforms in this way. If the term "agenda control" is to be used for both types of models, then the appropriate distinction would probably be between monopoly models of agenda control and competitive models of agenda control, where monopoly and competition refer to the nature of the agenda setter's position.

Conclusion

The agenda control literature is built upon a referendum model of government. A monopoly agenda setter determines the alternatives that the voters will face, although some limits may be placed upon the agenda setter's ability to specify alternatives. The most commonly evaluated limit is that the status quo must appear as an alternative to the agenda setter's proposal. The result is that the median voter's most preferred outcome is not offered in the referendum, and the agenda is manipulated so that a level of public sector output exceeds the level most preferred by the median voter.

Other types of agenda control to increase the public sector budget appear in the literature before the two-point offer referendum model, such as Buchanan's article demonstrating that the Bowen equilibrium budget will increase as the proportion of expenditures devoted to goods with more elastic demands increases. These models all have the common element that the median voter is forced to choose among a set of alternatives that does not include the median voter's most preferred alternative. These models can be considered models of monoply government in the sense that if there were competition for the position of agenda setter, a competing agenda setter could propose a platform that would defeat the existing agenda setter. A direct connection between the agenda control model and economic efficiency cannot be made, however, since the two-point offer equilibrium in the agenda control model is compared with Bowen equilibrium. The relevant comparison for purposes of evaluating efficiency is Samuelson equilibrium.

In contrast to these models of monopoly government are models of competitive government, where politicians offer the median voter a higher benefit/tax ratio in their platforms for elected office. The result is a lower per unit price of government for the median voter, causing the median voter to demand a higher level of output. The equilibrium budget increases in both monopoly and competitive models, but the crucial difference is that in the competitive models the budget is still a Bowen equilibrium, and the median voter is better off. In a model of political competition for position of agenda setter, monopoly agenda control would be discouraged and competitive agenda control would be encouraged.

Niskanen's model of bureaucracy falls somewhere between these two extremes, since the median voter gets the Bowen equilibrium level of output, given the biased information and superior bargaining position of the bureau. Niskanen equilibrium is consistent with Bowen equilibrium, although the two-point offer equilibrium in the agenda control model is not.

The next several chapters build upon the foundation laid in this chapter. Chapter 4 presents an empirical test that distinguishes the Bowen equilibrium outcome in referenda and compares it with the actual outcome. That test is followed by a discussion of some other empirical evidence on the median voter model. Chapter 5 then explains a referendum system that is guaranteed to produce Bowen equilibrium every time. The chapter includes applications of the referendum system to the real world. Chapter 6 develops a competitive voting model in which candidates may vary the tax shares of voters. This model is closely related to the concept of agenda control developed in the present chapter. Models of agenda control are relatively recent in the public choice literature, but they show great potential for explaining some of the more subtle aspects of democratic decision making.

An Empirical Test of the Median Voter Model

The median voter model has been one of the most useful analytic devices in public sector economics. When engaging in positive economic analysis, it provides a method for aggregating public sector demands into a single demand curve—the demand curve of the median voter. Even when evaluting the efficiency of particular equilibria, it is frequently convenient to summarize the preferences of all voters by expressing them as a distribution around the median. The median voter model is the public sector analog to the summation of individual demand curves to find a market demand curve in microeconomic theory. The model concludes that in a majority rule system, the demand curve that public sector suppliers face is that of the median voter.

The median voter model as it was originally depicted by Hotelling, Bowen, Black, Downs, and the others that developed it concluded that the median voter's most preferred outcome would be produced in a referendum. The possibility of agenda manipulation, described in chapter 3, casts some doubt on this conclusion. The agenda control model is still a type of median voter model, since the outcome of an election is determined by the preferences of the median voter, but in this case the outcome is not the median voter's most preferred outcome, but some multiple. The challenge that the agenda control model presents to the Bowen model is that the outcome of a referendum may be larger than the median voter's preference, although both models agree that the median voter is the only voter whose preferences count in determining the outcome of an election.

The election process depicted by the median voter model can be divided into three general categories: decision by committee, voter referenda, and election of representatives. The conclusions of the agenda control model are most applicable to the referendum models. Within a committee, any voting member is free to put forward a motion for consideration by the committee, meaning that the median voter's preference is likely to be voted upon. In the representative democracy model, continuous adjustment to the median is necessary to win the election, so although voters may elect candidates due to qualities other than their platforms and although candidates may not faithfully follow their campaign promises once elected, there still is a mechanism for continuous adjustment to the median in the model. By contrast, the referendum model can at best only approximate continuous adjustment, and if agenda setters decide to manipulate the choices available to voters, there is little recourse left to the voters. They must accept one of the offers tendered by the agenda setters.

Because the agenda control model is most applicable to issues decided by referendum, an empirical test based upon referendum results would be most likely to discriminate empirically between the Bowen model results and the agenda control model results. Accordingly, the empirical test presented in this chapter will evaluate the results of referenda. Some illustrations of cases of agenda control will be presented along with an empirical analysis of 257 referenda held in Michigan. Following the empirical test, some of the other empirical tests of the median voter model in the economics literature will be discussed in order to provide a more general overview of the correspondence between the median voter model and the actual referenda.

Public School Finance in Michigan

This section and the next will evaluate the results of some millage issue elections in Michigan during June of 1973.[1] In Michigan, each school district has a certain number of mills that it can levy without approval of the voters,[2] and any additional mills must be approved for a specific number of years in a millage issue election. After the millage levy expires, it must be reapproved by the voters before the levy can become effective again. Referenda could be held in a manner that closely approximate marginal adjustment, or they could be held in a manner to exploit any aspect of the two-point offer model which might exist. Concrete examples will probably illustrate this better than a lengthy explanation.[3]

Elections that are held for amounts that are small relative to the entire budget will have results that approximate marginal adjustments. The all-or-nothing portion of the offer can be only for a small increment. Furthermore, issues for millage renewal and issues for additional mills can be brought up as separate referenda, presenting the voter with a three-point offer and enhancing his opportunity to marginally adjust. For example, the residents of the Alma local school district were being taxed 23.30 operational mills[4] in 1972 and were presented with two separate referenda in June of 1973: the choice to renew 2.00 existing mills, and the choice to add 2.00 new mills. The millage renewal was approved by 69 percent of the voters, while the additional mills were favored by only 49.5 percent and were not enacted. Thus, according to the model earlier developed, Bowen equilibrium lies somewhere between 23.30 mills and 25.30 mills, and the school expenditures in the Alma district are very close to Bowen equilibrium.

This is illustrated in Figure 4.1. Since the second referendum received very close to 50 percent of the votes, the median voter was almost indifferent between the alternatives of 23.3 mills and 25.3 mills. This is shown using the concept of consumer surplus, where triangle abc is approximately equal to triangle cde. The median voter's most preferred millage rate is between 23.3 mills and 25.3 mills.

The Alma school district example shows that it is possible under the Michigan institutional structure to approximate marginal adjustment in school finance. The Springport local district provides an example demonstrating that the Michigan institutions will also allow the school board to increase the school budget, even when it is already larger than the median voter's most preferred budget. In 1971, the residents of the Springport district were paying 17.65 mills property tax and were given the opportunity to vote for an additional 2.00 mills. The issue failed. The next year, the electorate was presented with the single referendum to renew 10.00 mills and add another 2.35 mills, or to vote against both of these. The issue, then, was to approve the proposal and pay 20.00 mills, or to disapprove and be taxed only

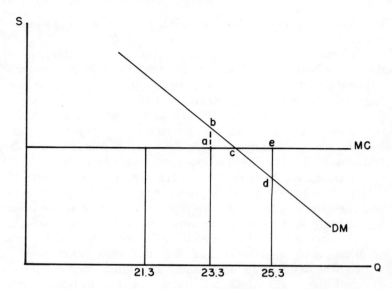

Fig. 4.1. The median voter in the Alma school district

7.65 mills. The issue passed by a scant 52.6 percent. Assuming that preferences did not change during the course of the year, the Springport school district was able to use the two-point offer aspect of the referendum process to offer voters a tie-in sale between renewal mills and additional mills in order to increase the budget beyond the level that would be approved if complete marginal adjustment were possible. In 1971, residents would not approve a marginal adjustment to a budget of 19.65 mills; yet in 1972, the residents agreed to purchase a tie-in sale of existing and additional mills which pushed the tax rate up to 20.00 mills. There is room for school boards to do some manipulation of the millage rates offered the voters in order to increase the level of expenditures beyond the Bowen equilibrium level. Figure 4.2 graphically illustrates this case in the same manner that Figure 4.1 illustrates the Alma case. The median voter is almost indifferent between 7.65 and 20.00 mills, and triangle abc is approximately equal to cde.

Keeping in mind the possibility of the two-point offer nature of the referenda, a number of other elections appear to be ex-

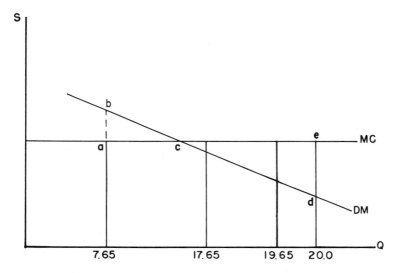

Fig. 4.2. The median voter in the Springport school district

ploiting the opportunity to increase the school budget beyond the level most preferred by the median voter. In the Bad Axe school district, voters were given the choice between approving a 10.75 millage rate renewal and being taxed 16.75 mills, or voting against the renewal and being taxed only 6.00 mills. The issue passed by 51.1 percent. When a large percentage of the total millage rate is being considered in the referendum, the opportunity for increasing the budget beyond the Bowen equilibrium level is increased. Apparently, the median voter in this election was almost on the margin, so that the degree to which the two-point offer model described the election process would indicate the amount by which the budget exceeds Bowen equilibrium.

These examples provide a general idea about the types of outcomes that could be expected in millage referenda. The referenda could be designed to approximate marginal adjustment, or they would be designed in order to extract the maximum tax payments from the voters by taking advantage of the two-point offer nature of the referenda. The next section will take a more detailed look at the referenda that were held in June of 1973 in order to discover the general character of the typical referendum.

Michigan Millage Referenda

The previous section described only a few millage elections in Michigan, giving some examples of possible election outcomes under the Michigan law. This section will evaluate the typical millage issue election by examining most of the elections held during June of 1973. There were 318 millage issue elections held during that month, and this section will use 257 of those elections as a data base for evaluating the operation of the Michigan system.[5] The focus of attention will be on the ability of the Michigan system to select the Bowen equilibrium level of expenditures. This focus appears to be the most relevant with respect to the existing literature, because of the frequent assumption that government expenditures approximate Bowen equilibrium. The assumption is particularly prevalent with respect to local government output.[6]

As was already noted, referenda may have some characteristics of the marginal adjustment model and some characteristics of the two-point offer model. Several reasons suggest that the two-point offer model is the more appropriate model for the Michigan data. First, the typical referendum considers 39.6 percent of the total operating budget. Because of the large percentage of the millage rate that appears in the typical election, the two-point offer model is probably a more realistic model for describing the referendum process than the marginal adjustment model. In addition, voters at one election do not know what alternative, if any, will be available at a later election. Thus, they may not see any opportunity of further alternatives in the event of a failure.[7] Also, voters could view repeated trips to the ballot box as costly, implying that transaction costs could inhibit marginal adjustment.

At this point, some additional assumptions will have to be made in order to draw conclusions relating to the ability of this institutional structure to approach a Bowen equilibrium solution. Two primary assumptions will be employed. The first is that demand curves are linear. The second assumption is that the preferences of the population of voters are normally distributed along the quantity dimension of the P-Q plane[8] and that the standard deviation of preferences is the same percentage of the median voter's most preferred budget in all school districts. That is, preferences in all districts have the same coefficient of variation. When these assumptions are incorporated into the millage referendum, the Bowen equilibrium millage rate can be located.

The first step in this process is the estimation of the standard deviation of preferences about the mean. The standard deviation was estimated by using these districts that held more than one referendum during the month. Twenty-four districts are in this category, and two of those districts held three elections during the month. Thus, fifty elections are in the sample from which the standard deviation was estimated. Referring to Figure 4.3, panel A, let the distance O'A represent the millage rate that would exist if the referendum fails, and O'B the rate if the referendum passes. When the second referendum is held, the millage rate in the event of a failure would be either O'A or O'B, depending on whether the first referendum passed or failed. In either case, the theory predicts that the higher rate of voter approval will be for the referendum that proposes the lower amount of mills in the event that the referendum passes. In four of the twenty-six cases, that condition was not met. Those four elections were dropped from the sample.[9]

For the remainder of the districts, the mean and standard deviation of preferences were calculated, using the two assumptions stated above. First, the two alternatives given the voters were recorded. The alternatives correspond to points A and B in panel A of Figure 4.3. Next, the percentage of yes votes was calculated, and that percentage was used to represent the voter who was indifferent between the two alternatives. Thus, if an issue passed by 60 percent, that voter for whom 60 percent of the people had higher demands than his and 40 percent had lower demands was used as the voter who was indifferent between options A and B. Assuming that his demand curve is linear, and because the benefits of the additional expenditure just offset the costs for this individual, the voter's most preferred quantity can be calculated as V, the point midway between A and B. The percentile and most preferred quantity of one other voter was calculated in the

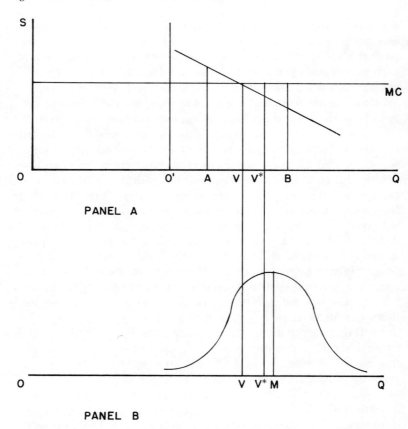

Fig. 4.3. Estimation of the median voter's most prefered referendum outcome

same manner, using the second millage issue election. The quantity can be represented by V* in Figure 4.3.

The points V and V* are two points on the assumed normal distribution of preferences. Associated with them are the percentage of yes votes in each election. Since preferences are assumed to be normally distributed, the number of standard deviations from the mean for both V and V* can be read from a table giving areas under a normal distribution curve. For example, if the election in which V was calculated passed by a 60 percent majority, then the voter who most prefers quantity V is the sixtieth percentile voter. A statistical table showing areas under the normal distribution indicates that the sixtieth percentile is about .25 standard deviations below the mean. This value is called S, the number of standard deviations that V is from the mean. In cases where more than half of the voters cast yes votes, S is the negative of the standard deviation, indicating that V is below the mean. S would be positive when less than half of the voters cast yes votes. A similar value, S*, is calculated to correspond to V*.

With these four values, the mean and standard deviation can be calculated algebraically. Equation 4.1 equates the ratios of the distance of V from the mean to the distance of V from V*, where M is the mean voter's most preferred millage rate. On the left side of the equation, the ratio is expressed in mills, and on the right side the ratio is expressed in the number of standard deviations from the mean. Solving this equation for M yields equation 4.2. The standard deviation in mills can then be calculated

$$\frac{V - M}{V = V*} = \frac{S - O}{S - S*} \tag{4.1}$$

$$M = V - (V - V*)\frac{S}{S - S*} \tag{4.2}$$

$$X = \frac{M - V}{S} \tag{4.3}$$

according to equation 4.3, where X represents the standard deviation in mills. Panel B of Figure 4.3 graphically demonstrates this calculation. When the number of standard deviations of both V and V* from the mean is known, the numerical value of M can be computed.

The model thus far has been concerned only with the local portion of the school operating budget, which is the marginal portion represented by points to the right of 0 in Figure 4.3. Individuals evaluate their satisfaction with the level of school expenditures based on the total budget, including state and federal funding; so inframarginal units OO' should also be considered in estimating voter preferences. The distance OM in panel B was arbitrarily assigned the value of 100, and the average standard deviation in the sample was 23.3. This figure was used as the standard deviation in all those districts that held only one millage issue election.

The calculation of the mean in those districts that held one election followed closely the calculation in districts with more than one election. Referring to Figure 4.3, the alternatives of A and B were offered, and the voter who preferred V was S standard deviations from the mean, where S is calculated as in the sample above. The mean demand is then calculated according to equation 4.4. Distance OO′ is added to the millage rate V in

$$M = \frac{V + OO'}{(1 + .233S)} - OO' \qquad (4.4)$$

the numerator, so that the numerator of the fraction represents distance OV. The denominator is the percentage that V is from the mean, expressed as a decimal fraction, so that the entire fraction in equation 4.4 represents the distance OM. Distance OO′ is then subtracted in order to express M as the number of mills that the mean voter prefers. Since the median and the mean are identical in a normal distribution, M is the number of mills most preferred by the median voter.

The median voter's calculated preference was then compared with the actual number of mills existing in every district. In the average district, the actual millage rate was slightly below the median voter's most preferred rate. The actual rate averaged 22.6 mills, while the median voter's most preferred rate was 24.1 mills. When this difference is converted from mills to dollars and calculated as a percentage of the average total operating budget, the average operating budget is only 2.4 percent away from Bowen equilibrium with a standard deviation of 13.5 percent. In terms of dollars, the average budget is $15.57 below the median, with a standard deviation of $107.94. Using a t-test to discover whether there is a statistically significant difference between the average actual budget and the average budget most preferred by the median voter, the t-value is .178, indicating that at the .99 level of confidence, there is no statistically significant difference. Therefore, the conclusion of this section is that the operational budget for public education in Michigan is close to the Bowen equilibrium budget.

Table 4.1 summarizes some statistics calculated from the Michigan millage issue referenda. The average referendum was approved by about 65 percent of the voters with a standard deviation of 13 percent. This suggests that in the typical election, the school board is not trying to find the largest budget that could possibly be approved by voters, but is looking for a level more closely in line with the preferences of the median voter. If school boards really are trying to exploit to the fullest the two-point offer nature of the referendum, then passage rates should be only slightly above 50 percent of the votes. This conclusion is reinforced by the fact that a relatively large percentage of the budget is considered in the typical referendum. In this sample, the average referendum considered over 20 percent of the average operating budget and nearly 40 percent of the total millage rates.

The conclusion that the operational budget for public education in Michigan is close to Bowen equilibrium can be explained in one of two ways. The first is that the referenda act as a constraint on the school boards which forces the budget to be held to the Bowen equilibrium level. As just noted, this does not appear to be the case in the sample just examined, since the passage

TABLE 4.1. Summary of Results from the Michigan Millage Issue Election Model

Statistic	Mean	Standard Deviation
Percent yes votes	65.3	13.4
Percentage of mills in referendum	39.6	23.4
Percentage of total operating budget in referendum	21.8	15.6
Average actual mill rate	22.6	5.5
Average median preference rate	24.1	7.2
Average actual operational budget divided by average median preference budget	.976	.135
Average actual operational budget minus average median preference budget	−$15.57	$107.94

rates are significantly greater than 50 percent. School boards might deliberately try to pass issues by more than a bare majority if they want to assure passage, in order to allow for some uncertainty in the outcome. Still, the evidence that the 65 percent approval rate is more than one standard deviation above 50 percent seems against the hypothesis that referenda act as a constraint.

A second explanation of the Bowen equilibrium result is that political competition for positions on the school board causes the board members to favor the Bowen equilibrium level of expenditures regardless of whether millage referenda are held. This explanation could be based on a Downsian model of political competition, but there is an additional reason for believing that this type of competition is effective in the production of education. Education is produced by local governmental competition. The taxpayer who believes that another school district provides a more desirable output for the amount of taxes to be paid has the option of moving to that district. This mechanism of adjustment would be most effective for individuals just moving into an area. One of the factors influencing the choice of residence will be the differences in educational services offered in each locality.

A more important aspect of intergovernmental competition might be the fact that each school board has another school board nearby which voters can use for comparision. If one school district spends significantly more on education than an adjacent district with little perceivable difference in quality, members of the first district would be inclined to replace their board at the next election. A board appearing to do well in comparison to nearby boards would be more likely to be reelected. Therefore, a school board has a good reason for comparing favorably with nearby school boards, regardless of whether or not millage referenda are held, and this mechanism of intergovermental competition might be effective in maintaining a school budget close to the median voter's most desired budget level. Political competition could have the effect of maintaining school budgets near Bowen equilibrium.

In summary, this section has used the result of millage issue referenda as a type of revealed preference experiment, and has found that the level of operational expenditures on public education in Michigan is very close to the Bowen equilibrium level.

The next section will examine the results of some other empirical studies. Most studies support the general conclusion that the public sector is in Bowen equilibrium, although some casual empirical evidence has suggested a budget larger than Bowen equilibrium in certain instances.

Other Empirical Evidence

Empirical models of public sector demands generally start by using the assumption of Bowen equilibrium rather than testing the assumption.[10] Nevertheless, there have been several empirical articles that have examined the assumptions of the median voter model, and this section will evaluate the results of those efforts. The empirical test in the previous section of this chapter is the most direct test of the median voter model because it is specifically designed to differentiate between the Bowen model and the agenda control model. By contrast, other studies have usually attempted to discover whether characteristics associated with the median voter are determinants of election outcomes. An example will illustrate this point.

One of the first serious attempts to verify the median voter hypothesis empirically was done by Barr and Davis in 1966.[11] After an exposition of the median voter model in mathematical terms, they assumed that the demand of the median voter for a number of public goods and services can be proxied by the per capita assessed taxable property value in a county and the ratio of owner-occupied residences to voters in the county. Using Pennsylvania data, they found that these variables were statistically significant in explaining the levels of expenditures for five groups of public sector goods and services. While several problems might be raised about their methods, the significance of this study is in attempting to test whether the characteristics of the median voter determine the outcomes of political processes rather than just assuming the median voter model to be true.

While the findings of Barr and Davis generally support the hypothesis that the public sector is in Bowen equilibrium, their test does not do much to differentiate the Bowen hypothesis from the hypothesis of agenda manipulation. The possibility remains that agenda setters might be able to increase spending above the

Bowen equilibrium level by an approximately constant proportion, meaning that while the outcome is a function of the median voter's demand, it is not the median voter's most preferred outcome. Any model that tests the Bowen hypothesis by testing whether election outcomes are a function of some characteristics of the median voter would be subject to this criticism. To say that the outcome is a function of the median voter's demand is consistent with the Bowen hypothesis, but it is consistent with some competing hypotheses as well.

With this problem in mind, Robert Inman's empirical test in his "Testing Political Economy's 'as if' Proposition: Is the Median Income Voter Really Decisive?"[12] goes a step further than Barr and Davis by calculating the difference between the outcomes of school referenda in Long Island and what the outcomes would have been if only the median income group had voted. More than simply finding a correlation between median characteristics and election outcomes, Inman tested whether the median income voter could be viewed as decisive, and could not reject the median voter hypothesis in any of his fifty-eight school districts at the .95 level of confidence. Inman's test provides better support of the Bowen model than the Barr-Davis test because it goes beyond simply finding a correlation between median characteristics and referenda outcomes.

Ultimately, though, Inman is testing a different proposition from the one tested earlier in this chapter. Inman tacitly accepts the conclusion that the public sector is in Bowen equilibrium and tests whether the median income individual can then be accepted as the median voter. His affirmative answer provides support for the median voter model, but does not demonstrate the public sector to be in Bowen equilibrium.

Another good test of the median voter model appears in McEachern's "Collective Decision Rules and Local Debt Choices: A Test of the Median Voter Hypothesis."[13] McEachern divides states into three groups based on the type of referendum needed to approve local debt issue: the first group requires no referendum, the second group requires the approval of a simple majority to issue debt, and the third group requires the approval of more than a simple majority. If local officials are elected according to the Downsian model of political competition, then they should propose the median voter's most preferred debt level without a referendum. The no referendum states should therefore be in Bowen equilibrium. In this case, holding a referendum requiring a simple majority approval of debt issue should not constrain local officials, so there should be no statistical difference between debt levels in the no referendum states and the simple majority referendum states. In states that require more than a simple majority—for example, 60 percent—the debt issue would have to be approved by a larger group; the sixtieth percentile voter will decide the issue rather than the fiftieth percentile voter. In those states, local debt issue should be smaller, which is what McEachern found. There is no statistically significant difference between local debt issue in the no referendum states and the simple majority states, but the states requiring an approval of more than a simple majority had a significantly smaller level of debt.

The empirical test presented earlier in this chapter has one unique aspect to recommend it as a direct test of the median voter model: it is the only one that directly estimates the median voter's demand and then compares it to the actual referendum outcome. As with most other empirical tests, the results support the hypothesis of Bowen equilibrium. Still, the model in this chapter has its shortcomings. For instance, the distribution of voter preferences is assumed normal and demand curves are assumed linear because no more information was available. The fact that other studies with vastly different methodologies support the Bowen equilibrium hypothesis is strongly favorable to the hypothesis, however. The general agreement of studies with different methodologies provides much stronger evidence than the results of any one study taken by itself.

One study that presents empirical evidence contrary to the Bowen model was reported by Romer and Rosenthal.[14] They are well aware of the limits of their method, and so caution that their empirical evidence is only suggestive, but it is certainly significant enough to warrant consideration. After explaining the agenda control model, they present evidence to suggest that in referenda, a lower reversion level will be associated with a higher referendum outcome. This clearly suggests (although does not prove) that the agenda controller is manipulating the referendum agenda. Although Romer and Rosenthal admit that more work needs to be done to substantiate empirically their hypothesis, their evidence makes clear that the possibility of agenda control exists, and that the agenda control model may best model certain referenda even if most elections conform to Bowen's model. It must be remembered that even in the Michigan data tested above, some individual districts appeared to tbe practicing agenda control even though the average district was near Bowen equilibrium.

Conclusion

The purpose of this chapter has been to examine from an empirical standpoint the concept of Bowen equilibrium within the median voter model. The main test described here used results from Michigan millage referenda to see if actual millage rates on average are significantly different from the median voter's most preferred rate. Due to data limitations, several assumptions were employed to derive the results. The most significant were that demand curves are linear, that the most preferred level of expenditures for all voters in a district are normally distributed, and that this distribution has the same coefficient of variation in all districts. Using these assumptions, the test in this chapter found that for the referenda analyzed, there was no statistically significant difference between the actual millage rate in the average district and the median voter's most preferred rate.

This result is especially significant since it implies that the referendum process takes into account the marginal preferences of voters. Some isolated examples demonstrated that the school board has the power to select referendum alternatives in a manner that would produce school budgets significantly larger than the budget most preferred by the median voter. Despite this power, the results presented here imply that the school board tends to select alternatives such that the median voter's most preferred alternative can be selective. This implies a mechanism of marginal adjustment in the political system, and the mechanism of marginal adjustment is crucial to many of the voter choice models now under development.

Coupled with results from other studies, there is a substantial amount of empirical support for the hypothesis that the public sector is in Bowen equilibrium. This certainly does not imply that in all cases the public sector is in Bowen equilibrium. Agenda setters may be constrained by the threat of losing their positions and so would attempt to produce Bowen equilibrium in the face of their upcoming bids for reelection. For this reason, it is important to recognize the limitations of the empirical test in this chapter. Since the public output examined was local education, there may be several reasons why the agenda setters would be more constrained than in state or national politics. For one thing, the agenda setters are members of a school board that provides only education, so the possibility for bribing various groups with different goods is limited. The agenda setters, for example, cannot promise more education to the education lobby and offset that by advocating more police protection to law and order groups and more welfare to other groups. This may constrain the school board (and if so would lead to the suggestion that at the federal level the secretary of defense, secretary of energy, and secretary of education be elected rather than appointed officials). In addition to this constraint, the fact that each school district is surrounded by many nearby school districts for comparison would further constrain school boards, who would want to look good by comparison.

In summary, then, while this one empirical test finds the public sector to be in Bowen equilibrium, additional empirical work in this and other areas of the public sector would be desirable to confirm or deny the hypothesis of Bowen equilibrium, particularly at the federal level where the political constraints differ markedly from local school finance. The upcoming chapters examine the concept of Bowen equilibrium from some different aspects. Chapter 5 describes a referendum system once used in Florida which always produces Bowen equilibrium, and chapter 6 illustrates that when tax shares can be proposed as a part of a political platform, there is the opportunity for the high demand of public output to increase expenditures beyond the level that would be produced with fixed tax shares. This gives politicians a method of manipulating the budget in addition to controlling the agenda, and may partially explain why little evidence of agenda control was found in this chapter.

The Florida System: A Bowen Equilibrium Referendum Process

The past several chapters have raised a number of questions (and perhaps answered a few as well) concerning decision making under majority rule. From the standpoint of economic efficiency, Samuelson equilibrium is the most desirable outcome of a public sector decision on the level of output to be produced, but majority rule institutions appear to have a Bowen equilibrium outcome engineered into their institutional structures. Chapter 3 examined the Bowen model in some detail and found that the potential exists for some manipulation of the outcomes of referenda so that perhaps referenda outcomes could be biased toward outcomes larger than Bowen equilibrium. However, the empirical test in chapter 4 showed that, at least for school referenda in Michigan, the results tended to be on average close to Bowen equilibrium. The issue about whether referendum results tend to be in general close to Bowen equilibrium will not be addressed in this chapter, however, because the Florida system is a referendum system that always produces the exact Bowen equilibrium result. This chapter will describe the operation of the Florida system and provide some historical background. Then, some issues concerning the general implementation of the Florida system will be discussed.[1]

Although the American system of government is frequently referred to as a majority rule government, the way in which the level of output in the public sector of the economy is determined varies with the type of output to be produced. Only rarely do individuals have the right to determine the quantities of output that they will consume. Instead, individuals in the consuming group must decide on a single level of output that will be provided to the entire group. This fact necessitates a group decision-making process that selects the public sector output to be provided to the group. Frequently, the group decision-making process consists of having individual consumers elect representatives, and the elected representatives determine the characteristics of public sector output. In some instances—most notably education—consumers are frequently given the opportunity to vote directly on some characteristics of the output bundle. A referendum is held where voters have their preferences aggregated according to specific rules, and the result of this aggregation process determines a characteristic of the public sector output bundle. Collective decision making through referenda has the advantage of supplying more accurate information about voter preferences, although the cost of decision-making in a referendum is higher than through representative government. Therefore, the use of a less costly and more accurate referendum process has the potential of substantially improving the responsiveness of governmental activities to the preferences of the voters.

The Florida system is a referendum system that was used in Florida to determine the level of operational expenditures in public elementary and secondary schools. The Florida system is a simple and elegant mechanism that automatically selects the level of expenditures most preferred by the median voter. Its interest extends beyond public school finance: the Florida system would be a good replacement for all existing referendum systems, and would be a quick and simple method of holding public referenda on many issues now decided by representatives. The Florida system will be placed in context by first discussing the differences in public school financing that exist in the various states of the United States.

The Institutional Structure of Public School Finance

The legal responsibility of providing public education in the United States rests with the individual states, so the institutional structure within which public education is financed is determined at the state level. These institutional structures vary considerably from state to state, although they have some common aspects. The most important common aspect for the purposes of this discussion is that the authority for producing education is delegated to local school districts. The institutional structure within which education is financed and produced is determined by the state laws, but the actual production occurs at the local level.

The states can be placed into three basic categories, depending on the institutions that they use to finance their operational expenditures.[2] In some states, school districts do not have the independent power to raise operational revenues, but receive funds from the general revenues of another governmental unit or units. These states can be called general fund financing states. In other states, school districts have the independent power to raise operational expenditures through an earmarked property tax, without the approval of the voters. These states are the earmarked tax states. In the third category, school districts have the independent power to raise operational expenditures through an earmarked property tax, but only if the tax levy is approved by the voters in a public referendum. Since the property tax rate is stated as a number of mills, these states are the millage issue election states.

Nine states and the District of Columbia finance education from a general fund. Nineteen states have earmarked local school taxes but do not hold millage issue elections. The twenty-two remaining states are in the millage issue election category. Within this category, there is a great deal of variation in the way in which referenda are held,[3] but the typical state holds referenda according to the following general principles. The school board proposes a certain addition to the millage rate, which is placed on the referendum ballot.[4] Voters then go to the polls; and the millage rate is either approved by a majority of the voters, in which case it becomes the effective rate, or it is not approved by a majority, in which case the old millage rate remains in effect. In the event that the new rate is not approved, school boards will typically propose a slightly smaller increase in the millage rate, and hold another referendum. This process continues until some rate is approved, or until voters have voted against even the smallest increase in the millage rate.

This process, then, is the Bowen equilibrium process described in chapter 2. The Bowen equilibrium result should occur without a referendum if school boards are elected, according to the Downsian model of political competition. Of course, there are a number of reasons why a Bowen equilibrium might not result from the election process, as explained in chapter 3. These reasons range from the possibility of agenda control introducing a systematic bias into election results to simply random errors in the agenda setter's estimation of the actual Bowen equilibrium quantity. The argument that Bowen equilibrium is not produced in a majority rule setting, however, is an argument that the political institutions are not operating as they were designed. But the institutions themselves, when working as they were intended, will produce a Bowen equilibrium. Bowen equilibrium is the object of a majority rule voting system. The earlier discussion in this book has already cast some doubt on the ability of existing political institutions to produce Bowen equilibrium. The fact or fiction of Bowen equilibrium in most political circumstances is open to debate, but the primary subject of this chapter is an unusual political institution that produces Bowen equilibrium every time. This political institution is the millage referendum system for financing public education in Florida. Millage referendum systems are generally close approximations of the median voter model, but the Florida system is unique in that Bowen equilibrium must be produced in every referendum.

The Florida System

The Florida millage referendum system automatically selects the Bowen equilibrium level of expenditures through the following process. Referenda may not be held more frequently than once in every twelve months, and voters are presented with the following instructions at the ballot box.[5]

> **INSTRUCTIONS TO VOTERS:** The proposed levy for the school term as proposed by the school board is 10 mills for operating expenses. Indicate your choice by making an "X" in the proper space below. If some other millage for operating expenses is desired, indicate by writing in the millage.
>
> ☐ **FOR** proposed levy of 10 mills for operating expenses.
> ☐ **AGAINST** proposed levy of 10 mills for operating expenses.
> ☐ Other millage levy ＿＿＿＿＿＿.

The tax rate receiving the majority of all votes cast then becomes the new tax rate. In the event that no one levy receives a majority, that levy which, together with the votes cast for higher levies, receives a majority of the votes then becomes the new tax rate. This method automatically selects the tax rate most preferred by the median voter.

If any one rate receives a majority of the votes, then the median voter must have voted for that rate. Less than half of the votes must have been cast on either side of the majority rate, since the majority rate was favored by more than half of the voters. If no single rate receives a majority, then that rate is selected for which half the votes were cast for that rate and all higher rates. This is the same as selecting the rate for which half the votes were cast for that rate and all lower rates, since the next higher rate and all rates above did not receive a majority of the votes. Therefore, the rate chosen is that rate most preferred by the median voter.

The Florida system has several advantages over the marginal adjustment systems that arrive at Bowen equilibrium. The most obvious advantage is that only one election is required to select the Bowen equilibrium rate of taxation. Also, in the marginal adjustment system described by Bowen, the margins could be wide enough to miss Bowen equilibrium by some amount. The Florida system guarantees exact Bowen equilibrium. Further, since only one election may be held each year, tactics such as threatening to eliminate high school sports or some other highly visible or desirable programs if a higher rate is not approved in the next election cannot be used. If the school board's proposal is rejected, the new millage rate is automatically determined for the next year, so there is no possibility of the school board's coaxing additional revenues out of the voters.

From the individual voter's standpoint, his choice is much the same as it would be in a millage issue election in any other millage referendum state. Since the school board's proposal appears on the ballot, the ignorant voter may select that level as the amount determined correct by the "experts," and the voter who knows little more than that the current expenditures are larger (or smaller) than he would prefer has a benchmark upon which to base his vote. Undoubtedly, the fact that the school board's proposal appears on the ballot affects the preferred millage rate of many of the voters, but this is not necessarily a drawback. As was just illustrated, it provides uninformed voters with a benchmark, while allowing more informed voters the opportunity to select the exact rate that they feel is appropriate.

A very important feature of this voting system is that it provides each voter with the incentive to reveal his true preference. It is a simple matter to instruct the voter to mark his most preferred tax rate, as the Florida ballot does. To design a system where it is in each individual's self-interest to reveal his true preference is a more intricate undertaking. The Florida system provides the proper incentives for each voter to reveal his true preference. If a voter's preference is above the median, his incentive is only to choose some rate above the median, in order to make the median as close to his preference as possible. His actual preference is as good as any other vote. Similarly, if the voter's preference is below the median, his incentive is to choose some rate below the median. Again, his actual preference is as good as any other vote. With all voters above and below the median having the proper incentives, the median voter will also have the proper incentive, since his preference will be selected. Thus, the voter can never cast a vote that will further his interest more than voting his true preference; and because there is some uncertainty before the votes are tabulated with respect to where the median lies, the voter could cast a vote against his self-interest by marking a tax rate other than his true preference. Therefore, it is in the best interest of every voter to mark his true preference on the ballot.[6]

Contrast the Florida system where the median vote is selected, with a hypothetical system in which the mean vote is selected. With this system, a voter whose preference was above the mean would have an incentive to overstate his preference, in order to raise the average. Similarly, a voter who preferred less than the mean would have an incentive to understate his preference and lower the average. The Florida system eliminates the possibility of strategic behavior that would further the interest of a voter.

In addition to providing the individual with the proper incentives, the Florida system is also very difficult for coalitions to manipulate. A coalition of individuals, all of whom desired a larger tax rate, could not strategically misstate their preferences in order to further their goal of raising the millage levy. All would vote above the median anyway; and aside from the median vote, the only significance of any vote in the tabulation process is that it is above or below the median. Thus, strategic voting by a coalition could not further the interest of the coalition.

Other potential collective choice systems find themselves more vulnerable to strategic behavior by coalitions.[7] The Florida system could be manipulated by an individual who bribed voters to switch from one side of the median to the other; but even here, the potential for manipulation is less than in the majority rule-type referenda. Under majority rule, the typical voter's vote does not matter, in the sense that the outcome of the election would remain the same with or without his vote. With the Florida system, each individual who casts a vote moves the median one individual closer to the voter, and thus slightly changes the outcome of the election (unless more than one person voted for the median rate). Thus, the individual's rate does change the outcome of the election, so an individual vote is more valuable to him under the Florida system than under majority rule.[8] An increase in the value of an individual vote might also have the advantage of increasing voter turnout, since each voter will realize a higher return from casting his vote.

In summary, the Florida system is an elegant means for selecting the Bowen equilibrium millage rate. The system is simple, and the individual voter is faced with a choice very similar to the voter in any other millage issue election. The incentive structure insures that it is in each voter's best interest to reveal his true preference. By holding only one referendum, the Florida system guarantees the selection of the exact Bowen equilibrium tax rate.

A Brief History

The Florida millage referendum system was instituted in 1939, and the referendum law still appears in the state code. The system is no longer operational, however; and a millage referendum has not been held in Florida in over fifteen years.[9] The reason for the demise of the Florida system is a provision in the Florida

Minimum Foundation Program which sets an upper limit on the number of mills that can be levied by participating school districts. The Florida Minimum Foundation Program, which provides state aid to local school districts, was instituted during the school year 1947–48. In 1968–69, a provision was added which required that districts not levy more than ten mills if they wish to participate in the program. In 1973–74, the Florida Minimum Foundation Program was replaced with the Florida Education Finance Act, which still provides a maximum millage levy. The present maximum is eight mills. Since school districts may levy this amount without a referendum, millage referenda are no longer held in Florida.

The result of this millage "cap" is to impose a more standardized level of expenditures upon Florida school districts. Individual districts cannot choose to increase their level of educational expenditures through higher local property tax rates without foregoing their state aid, and the historical fact is that districts do not forego the aid. The level of educational expenditures was decided at the district level in 1967–68, but is now determined at the state level.

During the last few years in which the Florida referendum system was effective, the degree to which school boards were able to select the Bowen equilibrium tax rate was astounding. Questionnaires were sent to each of the sixty-seven school districts in Florida, and forty-five replies were received providing data on eighty-five referenda during the years 1965–66, 1966–67, and 1967–68.[10] Of those eighty-five referenda, only ten selected millage rates other than those receommended by the school board. Of those ten, a rate below the school board's recommended rate was selected seven times, and a rate above the school board's recommendation was selected three times. According to these statistics, the school board must be considered quite successful in selecting the Bowen equilibrium rate. In other states, the rate of passage is not nearly so high.[11]

A More General Application

The Florida system is a simple and elegant means for selecting the Bowen equilibrium level of school expenditures. Only one referendum is required, and the exact Bowen equilibrium rate is selected. Since each individual's vote is more likely to change the outcome of a referendum in the Florida system than in the usual referendum process, voters will find their individual votes to be more valuable. Thus, a greater turnout would be expected under the Florida system than is currently observed. An additional asset to the Florida system is that the voter follows much the same process as in any other referendum, so an adoption of the Florida system in place of an existing referendum system would require almost no change in the procedure undertaken by the voter. The method of tabulation—not the method of voting—is the unique aspect of the system.

Because the Florida system is so straightforward, and because one referendum positively selects Bowen equilibrium, the Florida system would seem to be an ideal replacement for all existing referendum systems, and would also be a candidate for adoption in situations where the typical referendum process appears to be too cumbersome to be practical. Thus, voters could be offered many more opportunities to express their preferences than is currently possible.

The next section of this chapter will describe one possible method for extending the Florida system to more general referenda concerning the level of public sector output. An extension of this sort would be in the flavor of Wicksell's voluntary exchange model of taxation.[12] Wicksell's voluntary exchange model of taxation basically states that taxes are the price paid for public sector output, and that individuals should only be taxed to produce goods that provide net benefits in excess of the individuals' tax prices. There is evidence that some citizens do not view the present collection of taxes as in the spirit of the voluntary exchange model.[13] Some individuals, in fact, have suggested that the present system of taxation and spending amounts to taxation without representation.[14] The purpose of the next several sections of this chapter is to present a method of implementing tax reform in a manner that will remain responsive to the (perhaps changing) desires of taxpayers by allowing them to vote periodically on how their taxes are to be spent. The adaption of the Florida system would be simple enough not to require a sophisticated ballot from the taxpayer, and yet it should allow the taxpayer to determine both the aggregate size of the budget and how the budget will be allocated among functions.

The Tax Referendum

The taxpayer referendum could work in the following manner with respect to the Federal income tax.[15] At the same time that the taxpayer filled out his income tax form, he would have the option of filling out a ballot stating his preference on how the Federal budget should be spent. This ballot would list various categories of publicly provided goods among which the taxpayer could choose to allocate his vote. The taxpayer would also be given the option to vote for a refund of taxes to the group of taxpayers. Table 5.1 lists a sample hypothetical ballot. The voter has the option of voting for five goods, A through E, and a refund. The second column of the ballot shows the amounts currently allocated to each category, so that the voter can have a benchmark for voting. Another column could be included with a legislative recommendation further to provide the voter with information.

In the last column of the ballot, the voter can mark his own preference. With the other information on the ballot, the voter need know only a minimal amount in order to state accurately his preference. The voter might feel, for instance, that more money should be spent on category C, at the expense of category A, and can increase C some amount over the present allocation and reduce A accordingly. The voter is constrained to having all

TABLE 5.1. Sample Ballot

Goods	Present Allocation (%)	Legislative Recommendation (%)	Voter Preference (%)
A	20	22	19
B	30	30	29
C	10	9	9
D	25	26	24
E	15	13	14
Refund		0	5

categories add up to 100 percent. The voter in the sample ballot has voted 1 percent lower than the present allocation in all categories, and has voted for a 5 percent refund. This refund would not go directly to the individual casting the ballot, since the individual would have an incentive to vote too large a refund if he could determine his own refund. The next section will deal with the incentive problems.

Under this method of taxpayer voting, the taxpayer may choose how tax dollars should be allocated.[16] This type of ballot has the advantage that not only can taxpayers choose an allocation among public goods, but the taxpayer is also able to adjust on the margin between private sector and public sector spending. This gives voters the option of deciding whether the aggregate budget is too large, as would be suggested by current tax reform proposals. In short, the ballot requires little knowledge by the voter, but gives the voter an easy method for accurately expressing his preferences for public sector output.

Aggregating the Ballots

Two problems arise in aggregating the ballots. The first is finding a method of aggregation which gives each voter an incentive to reveal his true preference. This problem can best be illustrated by giving an example of an aggregation system that does not have this characteristic. Assume that the average voter preference for each category were used as the aggregate preference. This method of aggregation would invite strategic behavior. If a voter desired 25 percent of the budget to be allocated to category A, with reductions in all other categories, but felt that other voters would only vote 22 percent to category A, then the voter would have an incentive to vote 100 percent for A. With a large number of voters, he would not raise the average above 25 percent, but casting his vote in that manner would be the way to move category A as close to 25 percent as he can. The aggregation system should be designed in order to provide incentives for each voter to state his true preference.

The second problem is how the votes should be weighted. Each ballot could be weighted equally, the ballots could be weighted according to the size of the tax bill, or some other scheme could be used. Although practically significant, this problem is normative and will not be discussed further here.

A number of methods have been suggested for giving voters an incentive to reveal their true preferences.[17] Many of these methods require ballots more complicated than the ballot presented in the last section. The method suggested here would be to select the median preference for each category of goods. This method has the redeeming characteristic that voters have an incentive to reveal their true preferences. The only significance of a vote above the median is that it is above the median, so voters do not have an incentive to overstate their preferences as when the mean vote is taken. The converse is true of votes below the median, giving every voter an incentive to state his true preference.[18]

The aggregation process would work in the following manner, as illustrated in Table 5.2 in a simple example where the public sector provides three goods (one of which could be a refund). Individuals 1, 2, and 3 choose to allocate their votes as shown for the goods A, B, and C. The median is selected, which provides for 20 percent of the budget to be spent on A, 30 percent on B, and 50 percent on C. As long as voter preferences are symmetrically distributed about the median, the median votes will sum to 100 percent. If not, an adjustment may be necessary to have the totals sum to 100 percent.

One suggestion would be to sum the median preferences, and then divide the median for each good by this sum to adjust the median. In other words, where M_i^v is the median vote for the ith good and M_i^a is the adjusted median,

---

TABLE 5.2. Aggregating the Ballots: Example 1

Goods	Voters' Taxes (%)			Median	Median Adjusted to Sum to 100%
	1	2	3		
A	20	40	0	20	20
B	30	20	40	30	30
C	50	40	60	50	50

$$M_i^a = M_i^y / \sum_{j=1}^{n} M_j^y. \qquad (5.1)$$

This would leave the symmetric case in Table 5.2 unchanged, but would adjust the nonsymmetric cases in Tables 5.3 and 5.4 as shown. With a large number of voters, votes would be likely to be close to symmetric, so that adjustments should be rather small.

The advantages of this type of aggregation are that the ballot can remain relatively simple and at the same time can provide an incentive for each voter to state his true preference. In addition, ballots could be weighted in any manner, for example by the number of tax dollars. Any refund voted could be given in proportion to taxes paid, retaining the incentive to state true preferences.[19]

This discussion should not be taken as a suggestion about how an ideal referendum system would work, but rather as a framework for a workable system that could undoubtedly stand improvement. Discourse of this type must start somewhere, and

TABLE 5.3. Aggregating the Ballots: Example 2

Goods	Voters' Taxes (%)			Median	Median Adjusted to Sum to 100%*
	1	2	3		
A	20	10	80	20	22.2
B	30	50	10	30	33.3
C	50	40	10	40	44.4

*Percentage does not add to 100 because of rounding.

TABLE 5.4. Aggregating the Ballots: Example 3

Goods	Voters' Taxes (%)			Median	Median Adjusted to Sum to 100%
	1	2	3		
A	20	10	30	20	19.0
B	30	35	10	30	28.6
C	50	55	60	55	52.4

the system suggested here could be developed and implemented as a move toward the voluntary exchange model of taxation. Such an implementation must provide the voter with the proper incentives, as this one does, but it also must be simple enough so that the typical taxpayer can understand the process in order to cast a ballot that reflects his preferences. The system in this chapter seems to be a step in that direction.

Perhaps a referendum of this type could be held merely as a public opinion poll that would not constrain the choices of policy makers at all. This way, policy makers could have a direct reading of public opinion, and voters could have a direct reading on whether their elected representatives choose to follow public opinion. Even if used simply as a poll, this system would make government expenditures more responsive to the desires of the voters, moving closer toward Wicksell's voluntary exchange model of taxation.

Conclusion

The Florida system is a majority rule decision-making process that guarantees a Bowen equilibrium result every time, because it provides an incentive for voters to respond honestly and then selects the median vote. From an efficiency standpoint a Samuelson equilibrium would be preferable to Bowen equilibrium, but it is possible that the two may coincide. Still, in their ideal operations majority rule institutions select Bowen rather than Samuelson equilibrium. This may be due to the ignorance of the designers of such institutions, but there may be some reason why, at the constitutional level this type of decision-making rule is preferable. The evidence is its widespread use. At any rate, present majority rule political institutions are designed to produce Bowen equilibrium, and the Florida system is a referendum process that will generate a Bowen equilibrium with more accuracy than current majority rule institutions, and at a lower cost.

Other voting systems, demonstrated in theory but not in practice, will produce a Samuelson equilibrium if they are understood by the voters. The drawback of such systems as they presently stand is that they require the voter to convey significantly more information than present referendum systems. The

Florida system, by contrast, requires approximately the same information that the voter now conveys on the ballot. The distinction is in the method aggregating the ballots under the Florida system.

The Florida system is also relatively immune from strategic voting and vote purchasing to manipulate the referendum outcome. Not only does each individual have the incentive to vote honestly, but also it is not possible for a coalition of individuals with similar interests to vote strategically to manipulate the outcome of the referendum. The only aspect of an individual's vote that matters is on which side of the median it lies. It would be possible for an individual to be bribed into changing his vote, but even this is more difficult under the Florida system. If an individual were bribed to move his vote to the other side of the median, the median would move by one voter. Thus, every voter's vote has a marginal impact unless there is more than one voter casting the median ballot. This contrasts with the conventional referendum where no individual's vote counts unless the referendum is within one vote of a tie. Since the individual's vote is more likely to count, buying votes will be more difficult under the Florida system.

The Florida system was actually used for some years to determine public school expenditures in Florida. The system would be appropriate for much more complex types of referenda, however, as demonstrated in the later part of the chapter. A national referendum, with ballots to be cast along with income tax forms, would be easily accomplished. Even if the results were not binding, they would provide a good measure to policy makers concerning preferences about public sector spending.

Public Choice and Public Spending

The median voter model has been central to the development of the theme of this book. The evidence suggests that in majority rule politics the outcome of elections will in general be determined by the median voter's preferences. In the median voter model depicted by Bowen, Black, and Downs, an election is simply a process for selecting the median voter's preference. The Florida system, described in the last chapter, does the same thing more directly. The model of agenda manipulation depicted in chapter 3 still focuses on the median voter, for it is the median voter's preferences alone that provide the constraint for the agenda setter. Chapter 4 found that at least in some instances the Bowen model seems to explain referendum outcomes more accurately than a model of agenda manipulation. While the evidence does not generally support the agenda manipulation model, the evidence is on the basis of a small sample of elections, and all of a similar nature. Agenda control may be significant in other types of referenda, and even in the Michigan referenda there are isolated examples of agenda manipulation that are described in chapter 4. Agenda control is one way to manipulate the government budget, but there are other potentially more significant ways in which legislators affect the budget, and a subset of those ways will be the subject of this chapter.

One important observation about the median voter model is that the median voter must be informed about the available options and potential public sector decisions in order for every issue to be determined according to the median voter's preferences. Lack of information may often result from the rational behavior of voters who find it very costly to become informed about every issue before the legislature. As a result, special interests are able to convince legislatures to pass legislation favorable to the special interest groups. The concentrated group of beneficiaries is grateful and will support elected officials for reelection, and the diluted group of taxpayers has little incentive to become informed and put a halt to the special interest legislation. All these bits of special interest legislation add up, however, and as a result the total government budget (and the set of rules and regulations) becomes larger than optimal.

This phenomenon is well recognized and is the result of voters rationally remaining uninformed. The special interest phenomenon and the rational ignorance of voters are significant enough to warrant mention, but the main subject of this chapter is a bias in the political process in favor of large budgets which does not result from special interests or uninformed voters. To the contrary, the model in this chapter assumes that voters are fully informed about their choices and that the median voter's preference is chosen in an election. These other issues, which are certainly significant, will be assumed away in order to focus on a potentially important but little recognized bias in democratic decision making.

This chapter presents a simple model describing the political process that determines government spending in a democracy. The primary conclusion of the model is that political parties that represent individuals who desire relatively low levels of government spending will not be able to adhere to their principles and win elections at the same time. Under a wide range of circumstances, parties representing high demanders of government output will be able to construct a platform that will win a majority of the votes. The basis for the argument is the fact that demand curves are downward sloping. Both parties will find it in their interests to try to win the vote of the median voter by offering the median voter special tax breaks and special government programs. When the median voter receives this special treatment, that effectively lowers the price per unit that the median voter must pay for government output. When the price per unit of government output falls, the median voter will demand a larger amount of government output. When the quantity demanded by the median voter increases, his position moves away from the lower demand party and toward the high demand party. The mere fact that both parties are attempting to offer special benefits to the median voter causes the median voter's most preferred level of government activity to move toward the level most preferred by the high demand party. Incorporated into a framework of party behavior in a democracy, the median voter will favor the platform of the high demand party, and the high demand party will be elected.

This result is significant because of its contrast with the existing body of literature that uses economic theory to describe political decision making. The standard median voter model hypothesizes that the preferences of voters can be represented as existing along a continuum and that competition among political candidates will result in candidates moving their platforms toward the median. The model in this chapter depicts a somewhat different process, where changes in political platforms are made to try to alter the median voter's position along the continuum. The significance of the distinction between candidate movements and voter movements will be discussed later, after further developing the model demonstrating that a high demand party will have an advantage in attracting voters to its political position.

The basic model will be introduced with a simple case to demonstrate the mechanism of the model. The following section assumes that there are three groups of voters with high, median, and low demands for government output. There are two political parties: one representing the high demand group and another representing the low demand group. The party representing the high demanders will always be able to win the election. The median voter model suggests that both parties will tend to shift their platforms toward the position of the middle demanders, to win more votes. This model demonstrates that as parties adjust their platforms to converge on the median, the closer the parties get to the median, the more heavily the high demand party will be favored. With this brief introduction, the operation of the model will be demonstrated.

The Operation of the Model

This section will begin by specifying a set of simplifying assumptions within which the basic operation of the model can be seen.[1] Many of these assumptions will be relaxed later in the chapter, but the initial introduction of a very restricted model will simplify the exposition. This model hypothesizes that there are three groups of people in a society: a group that has a high demand for government output, a group that has a low demand for government output, and a median group that desires a level of output between the demands of the other two groups. Each group has an equal number of voters, and the demand curves of the three groups are assumed to be symmetrically distributed about the median. There are two political parties in this society. One party, party H, caters to the high demand group, and one party, party L, caters to the low demand group. Before each election, the parties formulate platforms that specify the quantity of government output to be produced and the tax share to be paid by each group. The outcome of the election is determined by majority rule, so both parties will try to capture the political support of the middle group in order to win the election and have their platform enacted.

Parties must follow two rules when formulating their platforms. First, each party must represent the demands of its group. The party must propose a tax and output bundle that sets the group's marginal tax price equal to the group's marginal valuation of government output. If a party does not follow this rule, then another party could arise which would better represent the voters. As long as parties follow this rule, no competing parties are assumed to arise.[2] Therefore, a party will find it in its self-interest to propose a platform along the demand curve of the group that it represents.

The second rule that parties must follow is that they must be equitable in their distribution of the tax burden. Within the context of this model, the equity rule implies that no party may propose a taxing arrangement that taxes another group more than it taxes its own. The party may propose to lower the tax price of one group; but to do so, it must increase its own taxes along with the taxes of the remaining group. For example, party H may propose to lower the tax rate of the median group in order to win the median group's support; but if party H raises the tax rate to party L, H must raise its own tax rate by the same amount. H can propose to tax any group at a lower rate than its own but cannot tax anybody a higher rate. To do so would be inequitable and would alienate voters.[3] Seen in a different light, this rule states that parties may lower the tax rate of one group by raising the general tax rate.

The operation of the model in its simplest case is illustrated in Figure 6.1. The horizontal axis measures the quantity of government output, which is assumed to be homogeneous Samuelsonian public good, and the vertical axis registers dollars. DH is the demand curve of the high demand group for government output, DM is the demand curve of the middle group for government output, and DL is the demand curve of the low demand group for government output. If politicians do not have the power to set the tax rate once they are elected, then party L would be constrained by the model to propose the level of government output at which DL intersects T1, and party H would similarly propose the level where DH intersects T1. Using a consumer surplus argument, DM would be indifferent between the two platforms.[4] A simple application of the median voter model, which does not consider the effects of tax-price changes, would predict that parties H and L would cease representing DH and DL in order to move toward the most preferred platform of DM and attempt to capture DM's votes and a victory in the election. This strategy will not be analyzed until the next section; the present will consider the case where both parties retain a platform on the demand curves of the groups that they represent.

The strategy that party H can use to try to capture the votes of DM is to raise the tax price of government to TH for DH and DL and use the additional tax revenues to lower the tax price of DM to TL, where $2(TH - T1) = T1 - TL$. Under this tax structure, party H's platform will call for Q_H output, and DM's most preferred level of output will rise from Q_1 to Q_M. DM would now vote for party H over party L. Party L could try to provide equally low taxes to DM; but the lower DM's tax rate becomes, the further DM's most preferred level of output moves from party L's platform. When parties charge equal tax rates to all groups, the median group will be indifferent between the two parties, as the standard median voter model would suggest. When parties try to win the approval of the median group by lowering the median group's tax price, the size of the government most preferred by the median group increases. This moves the median group's position away from the position of the low de-

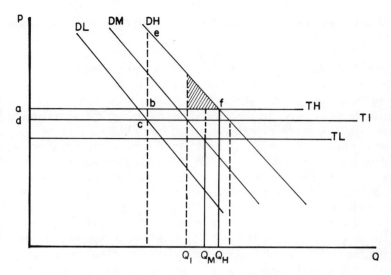

Fig. 6.1. The median voter model with variable tax shares

manders and toward the high demanders. If each party offers to lower the median voter's tax share by the same amount, party H will win the median vote and the election.

The advantage that the high demand party has in this model is a simple implication of the law of demand. When tax prices are shared equally among groups, the high demand party has no special advantage over the low demand party. When tax prices may be included as a plank in the party platform, parties may bargain for the median vote by offering the median group a lower tax price. The law of demand implies that when the price of government output falls, the quantity demanded increases, meaning that when both parties try to "purchase" the median vote through lower tax prices, the median voter will demand more government and move toward the high demanders.

Constitutional Tax Rules: A Digression

This model implies that under a system of variable tax shares that are determined by political entrepreneurs, the government budget will be larger than under a system of equal tax shares and that the political party catering to the high demanders of public output will have an advantage in being elected. The model does not imply that the high demanders will be better off with the system variable tax shares than under the system of equal tax shares. In Figure 6.1, when all voters pay the same tax price T1, Q_1 will be produced. The high demanders will be better off as a result of the consumer surplus gain from the increased output (which is the shaded area on the graph) but will be worse off due to the higher unit price they must pay for government output. There is no reason to believe that the consumer surplus gain from the larger output would be large enough to offset the loss due to the higher tax price, so the high demanders might prefer equal tax shares rather than the variable tax shares depicted in this model.

When tax shares can be varied, however, the best strategy for the high demand party is always to lower the tax share of the median voter rather than to propose equal tax shares. Under some circumstances, the low demand party will be able to offer the median group a tax break that it would prefer to equal tax shares. In this case, political competition will force the high demand party to offer the median voter a lower tax price with higher public expenditures, even when the high demanders would be better off with equal tax shares. If demand durve DL is sufficiently elastic and/or is sufficiently far from DM, there may be no platform that the low demand party could offer within the rules presented in the last section which the median group would prefer to equal tax shares. In this case also the high demand party will always have an incentive to provide a tax break to the median group. Without the tax break, the median voter will be indifferent between the two parties; thus, party H will have to use the tax break strategy in order to guarantee itself a victory. This will be true even though using such a strategy may make the high demand group worse off than if there was a constitutional rule mandating equal tax shares.

The high demanders may prefer removing the power to alter the tax structure from elected officials, but this would be a different issue from how tax shares would be set when they can be legally manipulated by politicians. A constitutional proposal to take the power to set tax shares away from politicians would be possible,[5] but then another bargaining problem arises. While high demanders may prefer a constitutional rule requiring equal tax shares, low demanders would prefer Lindahl prices to equal taxes. Since this problem is primarily a distributional one, there will be no one fixed set of tax shares that dominates any other if unanimous approval of constitutional tax shares is required. With majority rule, the bargaining process for determining constitutional tax rules would be the same as the bargaining process for determining tax shares in a party platform. The dominant strategy would be that described in the previous section.

Although there is one strategy that dominates all others, since the high demand party always has an incentive to offer a tax break to the median voter in order to win the election, there is not a dominant outcome that results from the election process. The high demanders will always prefer the smallest tax break to the median group, which would result in victory, since that would produce both the largest amount of government output and the smallest tax share for the high demand group. Under the special case where the low demand party is not able to offer the median group a tax break preferable to equal tax shares, the high demand party will offer the smallest tax break that the median group would find perceptibly different from equal tax shares. In other cases, the outcome is indeterminate.

Party Dynamics and the Median Voter Model

This section of the chapter will complicate the model somewhat in order to illustrate the consequences of the Downsian party strategy of moving toward the median. Figure 6.2 generalizes the model of the last section by assuming that there are fifteen voters symmetrically distributed about the median. Five voters are in the median group, represented by demand curves M1 through M5. Five voters each are also in the high and low groups, although only the demand curves of the closest to the median in each group appear in the figure. Voters more extreme than L5 and H1 will always vote with L5 and H1, so L1 through L4 and H2 through H5 can be omitted to simplify the diagram. In this model, party L will initially represent L5, and the party H represents H1. Once again, if tax prices are given at T1 for all voters, the median voter will be undecided in whether to accept Q government from party L or Q government from party H. By following the strategy of the last section, the parties can try to bribe the median voter by offering a lower tax price. Now, the entire median group will not have to be bribed, but at most only those between the median voter, M3, and the voter being represented by the party. Party H will offer lower taxes to M3, M4, and M5, while party L will offer lower taxes to M1, M2, and M3. As a result, taxes to the median voter will fall by four times the amount that the taxes of party members are raised, and M3 will increase his quantity demanded from Q to Q_1 and will vote for party H. As before, party H will win the election.

Recall from the last section that a larger tax reduction offer from party L will increase the quantity of government demanded by M3. An identical tax offer by party H would again mean victory for H. The median voter model suggests that in the process of political competition, parties will tend to move toward the me-

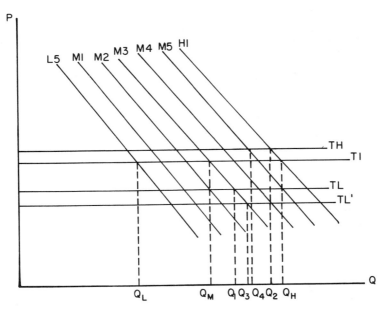

Fig. 6.2. The variable tax share model with more voters

dian. If party L moves inward to represent M1, and party H replies by representing M5, the result is even more extreme. Fewer voters need to be bribed, so the same tax rate TH to the party members will lower the median group's rate to TL', so that M3 will now demand Q_3. Party H will win, but will only provide Q_4 rather than Q_2 output. As parties move closer to the median, a victory for the high demand party becomes more certain.

Placed within Down's density function framework in *An Economic Theory of Democracy*, the model of this chapter implies a shift in the density function as tax shares are altered. Figure 6.3 illustrates the point. Voter preferences are ranked along a single dimensioned continuum of government size. With equal tax shares, the density function of voter preferences appears as the solid curve. The median voter most prefers that level of government where the solid vertical line intersects the axis; and if tax shares are not variable, that is the level of output that will be produced. When tax shares can appear as a plank in party platforms, the process of lowering the tax share of the median voter causes his most preferred level of government to rise. The median voter's most preferred level of government then shifts to that level represented by the intersection of the dashed line with the axis. The dashed density function represents the new distribution of voters. Using the density function approach, the model can be generalized to any number of voters.

This model can also be generalized to the case where government output is not a homogeneous public good, but where there are many outputs of government, some providing substantial private benefits to some groups. In this case, instead of applying the increased tax rates of some groups to provide lower tax rates to the median group, all tax rates could be increased, and the increase could be used to provide essentially private benefits to some groups. For example, taxes could be used to buy food for some people, as in the food stamp program, or housing, as in the subsidized housing in urban renewal programs. These types of benefits simply substitute for housing or food expenditures that recipients would have had to make in the absence of the government transfer and so amount to a simple income transfer. Thus, the per unit cost of government is decreased to the recipients of these private benefits, and the effect is the same as in the case where the individuals are given tax cuts.

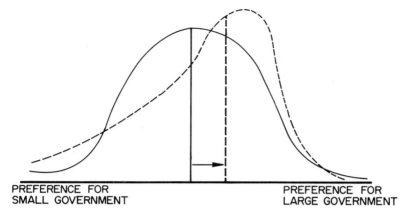

PREFERENCE FOR
SMALL GOVERNMENT   PREFERENCE FOR
                                                   LARGE GOVERNMENT

Fig. 6.3.   The variable tax share model in a density function framework

The result of this model would not necessarily hold in the
case where the special program provides benefits to individuals
that they would not ordinarily provide for themselves. An example would be national defense. In this case, the median voter
may prefer a larger or smaller quantity of government output,
depending upon whether his marginal valuation for the special
program is above or below his marginal tax price of the program
at the quantity that he would most prefer without the special
program. That is, if the individual's taxes had to be increased to
pay for the special program, he would have to value the output
of the program more highly than his tax cost.[6] Income transfers
are simply a special case where the recipient always values the
output more highly than the cost, since the recipient's group pays
only a portion of the tax price but receives the entire amount as
income. Thus, a high demand party should always be expected
to favor special programs that are essentially income supplements, because income supplements are analytically equivalent
to a tax cut and will reinforce the movement of the median group
toward the high demand group.

While the high demand party has an incentive to provide
income supplements to reinforce its advantage in winning elections, the low demand party does not have this incentive. By
providing certain types of public goods, the low demand party

may be able to increase the well-being of the median group while lowering its marginal value of government output. Assume that the public good to be produced is a television broadcast station, which has the Samuelsonian publicness characteristic that an additional viewer can turn on his set and not detract from the signal received by any other viewer. If the three groups of voters live in three distinct neighborhoods, the optimal strategy of the low demand party may be to locate the broadcast antenna in the middle demand neighborhood. With a relatively weak signal, the middle demanders will be able to receive a good picture and will not desire much additional output (wattage), whereas the other groups who live farther away will pick up a weak signal and may desire greater government output from the station. By strategically placing the station, the total value of government output to the median group increased, but the marginal value declines, moving the most preferred output of the median group toward the low demanders.[7]

Tax cuts and income transfers are analytically equivalent in this model, but the provision of public goods that would not ordinarily be provided individually may favor the low demanders. Thus, the high demand party would be more likely to favor special programs that are essentially income transfers, whereas the low demand party would be more likely to offer programs of a more public goods nature.

The Optimal Strategy for the Lower Demand Party

The basic mechanism of this model operates through parties offering lower tax prices to the median voting group by charging higher tax prices to everyone else. The party thus offers to spend some of the consumer surplus that it would receive from its platform of governmental activity on influencing the median group to vote in its favor. The rational party should wish to apply as little of its consumer surplus as possible toward winning the votes of the swing voters. This fact leaves some hope for the lower demand party.

If the lower demand party commits itself to a platform offering very few (if any) special favors for the median group, then the high demand party can win the election by offering the median group a relatively small amount of special benefits. The lower demand party could then try to switch its platform to one offering a large amount of benefits to the median group, in an effort to defeat the high demand party's relatively weak platform. There are several problems with this strategy. First, the high demand party could always change its platform to one which could defeat the lower demand party, no matter what platform the lower demand party picks. Furthermore, parties that have a record of making drastic changes in their platforms may lose credibility as well as voters. Thus, parties may find it disadvantageous to change their platforms once they have committed themselves.

The lower demand party should therefore try to imply that it will not pick its strongest platform, without actually committing itself. If the lower demand party can wait long enough, the high demand party might commit itself to a platform that will defeat the implied platform of the lower demand party. Then the lower demand party could reject its implied platform in favor of a platform that will defeat the platform of the high demand party. Such strategic behavior, as well as the lack of firm commitment to a platform for a long period of time, may be viewed with distrust by the voters. Still, if the lower demand party is the first to commit itself firmly to a platform, it is sure to be defeated. In order to win the votes of the uncommitted voters, the lower demand party must lure the high demand party into thinking that it can win the election without using its most powerful platform.

Democrats and Republicans: Subsidizing the Poor

The model of this chapter could be applied to the current American political scene, where the Democrats represent those individuals with a high demand for government output, and the Republicans are the lower demand party. The parties are trying to formulate their platforms in such a manner as to win the vote of the median voters, who might be poorer individuals who are not strongly associated with either party. In this case, the poor should be expected to receive special programs in party platforms to try to win the poor vote.

The conclusion of the model is that if both parties offered equal subsidies, the Democratic party would have the advantage in winning the election. The model would therefore predict that more Democrats than Republicans would be elected. The model would also predict that the Democratic party has an incentive to offer special programs that amount to income transfers in order to win the poor vote. This is in fact what has happened. The poor are offered low income housing, food stamps, and medical care, which are all items that would otherwise be purchased from the consumer's budget. Similar offers by the Republicans could always be defeated by a Democratic platform, so the model would expect Republican platforms to be geared more toward public goods in the Samuelsonian sense: things like national defense and foreign relations.

The implications of the model explored in this section suggest that Democrats should get elected more often than Republicans and that large government budgets with large income transfers to the poor should be expected as a matter of political expediency. In a democracy, politicians find it in their self-interest to subsidize the poor, if the poor represent the swing voter. The argument in this section provides a rationale for poverty programs other than that some people like to do nice things for other people.[8]

The Impossibility of a Libertarian Democracy

One implication of this model is that a Libertarian political party, which represents the low demanders of government output, will not be able to adhere to its principles and win elections at the same time. This implication follows directly from the conclusion of earlier sections, where the party representing the high demanders of government output was demonstrated to have the advantage in winning elections. A related implication that is a bit more subtle is that a strengthening of a Libertarian movement will actually cause an increase in the level of government expenditures. This is true because the lower the demand of the party opposing the high demanders, the closer the swing group's preferences will be to the preferences of the high demanders.

This implication can be seen within the model as depicted in Figure 6.2. When parties took relatively extreme positions, representing L5 and H1, the amount of government output produced was Q_2. When the parties converged toward the median, representing M1 and M5, the high demand party had to lower the amount of output that it proposed, and Q_4 was produced. Thus, the closer party platforms are to the median, the lower the level of government output. If the lower demand party selects a more extreme position, this will enable the high demand party to move farther away from the median and enact a larger-sized government than if the lower demand party were closer to the median. Thus, given a distribution of voters, the more extreme a Libertarian party becomes, the larger the government will be.[9] Ironically, the formalizing of a Libertarian movement in this country might actually cause an increase in the size of the government.

At this point, a corollary on Libertarian tax proposals can be developed. A high demand party has an advantage in giving tax breaks to lower demand groups in that, by doing so, the quantity demanded by the lower demand group rises and comes closer to the quantity demanded by the high demand group. This same principle works to the disadvantage of a low demand party trying to offer a tax break to a higher demand group. When a low demand party offers such a break, the quantity of government demanded by a higher demand group moves away from the low demand position. The higher demand group would even be against such a lowering of its tax rate under some conditions, since it would also mean a lower quantity of government. Under some circumstances, any reduction in taxes that could be offered by a Libertarian party may not be able to compensate voters for the smaller-sized government they would have to accept. Thus, it is always in the interest of the high demand party to offer a tax break to the median voter in order to convince him to accept a higher output of government; but, depending on the distribution of community preferences and the elasticity of the median demand, the median voter may most prefer no tax break to a tax break, if lower taxes implies a lower government output. Therefore political parties representing high demanders of government will favor tax provisions and "loopholes," whereas low demanders would prefer uniform tax rates for all. This may be the result of ideological convictions, but it is also a rational step toward political popularity.

Political Behavior in a Democracy

The model in this chapter emphasizes an important characteristic of democratic decision making: the individuals who care the least about the outcome of a decision are those who determine the outcome. Individuals who have strong preferences for one party or another have already committed their votes. It is the voter who does not strongly prefer one alternative to another who may vote either way and who therefore may affect the outcome of the election. Voters who have the strongest preferences never cast the decisive votes; the voters who care least about the outcome of a decision cast the votes that count the most. This fact might frequently lead to "random" decisions, in the sense that the decisive voter makes his choice on the basis of something other than the platforms he chooses between, were it not for the type of behavior posited in this model. Downs has shown that, under any circumstances, voters have little incentive to become informed about the political choices they face. This is especially true of the median voter.

To avoid a "random" decision-making process, parties will attempt to offer special programs to benefit the median voter. The decisive voter will then favor the party that offers him the most attractive special programs. The fact that these programs appear in a democracy is commonly recognized. The implication of this analysis is slightly different from the standard interpretation, however. Special programs are not offered as favors to the individuals who are strong party supporters. The strong supporters may actually find themselves receiving less from the government than if there were no special programs. The net beneficiaries of the programs are the weak party supporters, who would support the other party in the absence of the reigning party's favors. Politicians are restricted in the amount of private benefits that can be granted for their strongest supporters. The consumer surplus generated by being elected must be used, in part anyway, to convince more neutral voters to vote for the party.

Conclusion

The party that can offer the most favorable platform to the median group of voters is the party that will be elected. An effective way of winning the median vote is to offer the median voter a special package of taxes and/or government programs. In order to do this, parties must sacrifice some of the consumer surplus that they would get from what they would consider an ideal platform and instead give benefits to the median group. If both parties are willing to raise general taxes by the same percent in order to give special benefits to the median voter, then the party that represents the high demanders of government output will be able to win elections over the party representing lower demanders. The result is that a democracy has a natural bias in favor of electing the political party that has the highest demand for public sector output.

The standard median voter model goes a long way toward explaining observed political behavior within an economic framework. However, the median voter model generally assumes that tax shares are given. This chapter has demonstrated that when different distributions of tax shares can appear in the political platforms of parties seeking election, the model goes a bit farther in explanatory power and also has some interesting implications not contained in the model assuming fixed tax shares.

Elements of Monopoly in Government

In textbook explanations about some shortcomings of the market system, one shortcoming that will almost always be cited is the potential for monopoly.[1] Yet in governmental production, the public sector producer is almost always a monopoly producer. This may be because the government allows use of the output without charge, as in the case of roads. Few people then have the incentive to compete. Or it may be, as in the case of the United States Postal Service, that the government has simply made competition illegal. In fact, there seems to be a general policy of centralization in the government that is just the opposite of the policy of decentralization applied to the private sector. In the private sector, decentralization means competition, which is the official government policy as the antitrust laws will attest.[2] This policy is just the opposite in government, where centralization is pursued in the name of eliminating duplication of effort. The Department of Energy was formed under this premise. Governmental programs dealing with energy were spread among many departments, and this decentralization and competition among arms of the government was viewed as undesirable, so competition was eliminated by centralization, and the Department of Energy was born.[3]

This is one aspect of monopoly in government. Government programs tend to have no competitors, either from within or outside the government. But there is another aspect of monopoly in government that is inherent in the nature of majority rule politics: once elected, the political official has a monopoly on that political office for a specified period of time. For this reason, the production of political outcomes has some characteristics of a natural monopoly. The second aspect of monopoly in government, then, is the monopoly acquired by majorities through the political process. This monopoly power may be the base from which the agenda setters who played such an important role in the agenda control model of chapter 3 derive the power to control agendas. At any rate, the monopoly power inherent in majority rule politics must be recognized.

The first part of this chapter will examine some monopoly aspects of political parties. Then, some monopoly aspects implied in incumbency will be examined. This material is directly related to chapter 8, where some constitutional issues in majority rule are examined. Then, some remarks will be made about monopoly bureaus in the context of the Niskanen model.

Monopoly Aspects of Political Parties

In a political system where policy outcomes are determined by a majority, the majority coalition is the single producer of political decisions.[4] This majority coalition is analagous to the single firm in a natural monopoly. The coalition's "majority" is its indivisible asset that acts as a barrier to entry to other coalitions desiring to produce political decisions. As Tullock noted, "The natural monopoly here comes from a technological consideration which amounts to a very strong economy of scale: only one majority can exist at a time."[5] As a result, once a coalition has a majority, which is a costly and indivisible asset, it can produce legislation at a marginal cost below average cost. The average cost includes the cost of acquiring a majority, but once the majority is acquired, the marginal cost of producing legislation is very low. This observation applies any time a majority is required to affect a political action. It applies to electing representatives to legislatures, as well as to legislative decisions themselves that are made by majority rule. The model here, though, will develop some implications of the natural monopoly argument by applying it to political parties.

In order to produce majorities, coalitions appear in the form of political parties and use resources to produce their output in the same way that firms use resources to produce output. Because the majority owned by the successful producer is an indivisible asset, parties will view their average cost curve as downward sloping, with marginal cost below average cost, in the same way as would firms in any other natural monopoly. Thus, the calculus of the political party can be depicted by the curves in Figure 7.1.

The quantity axis measures the production of political outcomes. Political outcomes are produced when the majority coalition approves the passage of legislative measures. In effect, the production of political outcomes can be viewed as a two-stage process. The acquisition of the majority asset first involves costs which are incurred during the periodic rivalry for election. At this stage coalitions compete for the field by devoting resources to political campaigns. That is, they compete for the property rights to supply political products during the legislative session. This stage of the political process involves substantial costs in the form of campaigns to place party members in elected offices. These costs are necessary for the party that wishes to produce legislative output, since only successful competitors are granted the right to produce output. At this stage, no output is produced, but the winner is granted the exclusive rights to production during the legislative session. The second stage of the process is the legislative session, which starts anew after each election and is the actual period of political production. The costs incurred during the period of production, then, are the resources devoted to passing legislative measures.

Once the majority asset has been acquired by a coalition, the marginal cost of securing approval of an additional measure is approximately constant. The cost to the majority of producing another measure involves drafting potential legislation, introducing a bill into the committee process, disseminating information about the bill, and bringing it before the legislature for discussion and a vote. Because all political outcomes are subject to the same processing and approval procedures, the marginal cost of producing additional legislation—once a majority coalition exists—will remain approximately the same.

Since there is a fixed cost involved in producing the majority necessary for the production of the first legislative outcome and since the marginal cost of producing additional outcomes is constant, the average cost to the majority coalition of producing legislative outcomes is declining and lies above the marginal cost. The quantity axis in Figure 7.1 measures the number of legislative outcomes produced by a coalition, given that the coalition

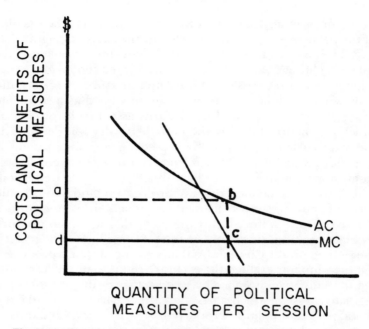

Fig. 7.1. The cost of producing legislative outcomes with decreasing party costs

has already produced the majority asset. The corresponding costs and benefits of producing legislative measures are represented on the vertical axis.

The size of the majority will affect its value if the marginal cost of producing legislation is lower with a larger (say, 65 percent) majority than with a smaller (say, 55 percent) majority. For any given size of the majority, however, the marginal cost of producing outcomes will remain constant. And although a larger majority results in a parallel shift downward of the marginal cost curve, the fixed cost of producing a larger majority would be greater.[6] Hence, the effect of different-sized majorities on the average cost of producing legislation is indeterminate on a priori grounds.

The party will have some marginal valuation schedule for the production of political outcomes, but since the party can only spend the funds it raises, the party will be constrained to produce at the point where its marginal evaluation curve intersects average cost, rather than where marginal valuation intersects the marginal cost curve. The party would prefer to produce where marginal cost equals marginal valuation, but in order to do so it would have to be subsidized by the amount represented by quadrangle abcd in Figure 7.1.

Political parties therefore have the incentive to seek subsidies in order to expand their output to the point that satisfies the marginal conditions for optimality. The presidential campaign contribution checkoff on income tax forms was initiated by politicians to provide lump-sum subsidies to political candidates in an attempt to satisfy these marginal conditions. The funds collected from the presidential checkoff are divided among all candidates who collect at least $2,500 in contributions of $250 or less in at least twenty states. To the candidate who meets these conditions, his share of the funds collected from the checkoff will be treated as a lump-sum subsidy, enabling party production to expand. The existence of this lump-sum subsidy is evidence in favor of the natural monopoly hypothesis.[7]

In the absence of the declining costs hypothesized in this chapter, political parties would not desire a lump-sum subsidy. Political parties are nonprofit organizations and therefore cannot benefit from having average cost lie below marginal cost. A lump-sum subsidy would lower the average cost to parties of generating majorities, but would not effect the marginal conditions for producing legislation. Therefore, the optimal amount of output would remain unchanged. This point is illustrated in Figure 7.2, where the increasing cost case is drawn.

A lump-sum subsidy to a profit-making firm would lower the average cost to AC', so that the firm would be able to appropriate rectangle abcd as profit. The nonprofit political party would not be able to appropriate this surplus, however, and so it would behave as if the subsidy displaced inframarginal funds shown by the rectangle aefo, which is equal to the area abcd. The effect of a lump-sum subsidy would be to displace some party resources in producing the inframarginal units, while the remainder of the party continued satisfying the same marginal conditions as before the subsidy. The subsidy would make the party smaller, but would not affect the total amount of resources devoted to producing a majority. In effect, the subsidizing agency would replace a portion of the party in the absence of decreasing costs.

A reasonable assumption is that political parties prefer a larger size to a smaller size. Evidence that political parties are seeking lump-sum subsidies would therefore support the hypothesis that political parties have declining-cost functions, but would be at odds with the hypothesis that they have constant or increasing costs.

Given this explanation of the recently approved subsidy to political campaigns, the question then arises about why parties did not seek this subsidy before. The campaign subsidy was approved along with a measure to limit personal campaign contributions to $1,000. Before this contribution limit was passed, parties had the power to price discriminate by charging different

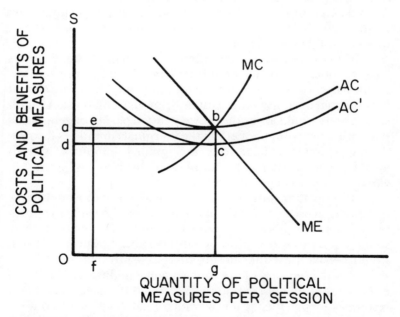

Fig. 7.2. The cost of producing legislative outcomes with increasing party costs

prices to different supporters for the same party platform. The price discriminating natural monopolist would be able to price along its marginal evaluation curve, and thus could satisfy its marginal conditions for optimality without a subsidy. By setting a limit on individual campaign contributions, the party lost a great deal of ability to price discriminate, and should therefore desire the subsidy in order to compensate for the loss of the ability to price discriminate.

While most monopolies would relish the opportunity to price discriminate among their customers, political parties may not find the opportunity quite so enticing. For one thing, larger contributors may have more influence over the party, and party officials would have good reason to view this as undesirable. By limiting the size of campaign contributions, parties will have more independence from large backers. For another thing, the party's competitors will lose the ability to price discriminate also, and since parties are competing for a fixed number of seats, no individual party would be worse off.[8] the point is, however, that political parties, unlike most firms, may have good reason to eliminate the ability to price discriminate among potential customers, since the party will then be less under the influence of large contributors.

The Firm and The Industry

There is evidence that the rational declining-cost "firms" in this industry are attempting to receive a lump-sum subsidy, and ordinarily, an economist's prescription in the case of declining costs would be to subsidize. But there is a difference between the firm and the industry and, in this case, the industry does not exhibit the same declining costs as the firms in the industry. The firm is attempting to produce political decisions, but these decisions will be produced regardless of the amount of money devoted to obtaining the indivisible factor of production—the majority. With a two-party system, one party will have a majority in any event.

The problem in this industry is that firms generate externalities upon each other in the process of production. The party's return in any election will be somewhere between 0 and 100 percent of the vote, and for every percentage point that a party produces for itself, it reduces the percentage for the other party by an equal magnitude. The firm, of course, does not take account of this external cost in determining its level of output.[9]

This externality is a technological rather than a pecuniary externality. The additional funds spent by parties as a result of the externality are not merely devoted to bidding up the prices of resources already used in the industry; rather they are spent to purchase additional resources for use in campaigns. The externality is technological since additional resources, not just money, must be used by one party to hold its output constant when the other party increases its expenditures.

As a result of this externality, there will be too many resources devoted to producing majorities. In the absence of subsidies, the declining-cost characteristics of the firms will keep them from producing at the point they would consider optimal, but even this level of expenditure will probably be excessive, since in a system of majority rule a majority could be produced with no expenditures. As long as some individuals vote, one party will receive a majority.

There is a positive externality generated through campaign expenditures; the dissemination of information about political candidates. This information is strictly a by-product of the expenditures, though, since parties expend money to elect their candidates and not to act as information services. Given Downs's conclusion that voters have little incentive to become informed, and given that people follow the news to some degree, the information generated by political campaigns may have little or no value. In fact, if information generated by the news media is more accurate, then campaign information may even have a negative social value.[10]

The standard economic model of a natural monopoly offers a useful conceptual means to examine some of the characteristics of political parties. The declining-cost curves for producing political products are attributable to the indivisible nature of the majority asset. In the absence of subsidies, political parties can be expected to produce at the point where their marginal evaluation equals average cost. Thus, they have the incentive to seek subsidies in order to expand production to the point where marginal evaluation equals marginal cost. While this is optimizing behavior on the part of the individual party, it may not be optimal in competing for the majority asset, because this process decreases the value of resources that the other party has expended toward acquiring the asset. Parties will determine their optimal output calculating only the private costs and benefits, but will ignore the social cost caused by the externality they generate. As a result, optimizing behavior by the individual parties may lead to an excess of resources devoted to producing political decisions.

Competition Between Incumbents and Nonincumbents

Competition between political parties is an obvious form of political competition, and an obvious way to delineate sides in political battles. However, a very significant type of political competition, and one that has certainly not received enough attention, is competition between incumbents and nonincumbents. On the surface, competition between incumbents and nonincumbents might be easily obscured, because when a nonincumbent challenges an incumbent the final contest will almost always be between two individuals of different parties. The most visible competition tends to be centered upon party ideology and differences between candidates, and thus appears as party competition. The incentives for competition between incumbents and nonincumbents are strong, and so the implications should be analyzed.[11]

Of course, incumbents will always face nonincumbent challengers, but the real question is how coalitions form in the political competition. In general, incumbents have an incentive to approve measures that will strengthen the ability of incumbents to be reelected. This common incentive causes incumbents in general to favor legislation making it harder for challengers to defeat incumbents, and thus results in a coalition of incumbents against nonincumbents.

In fact, lines of political competition are probably more clearly drawn in this dimension than along party lines. Incumbents already have tremendous advantages in being reelected, as a result of greater news exposure as well as items such as government travel allowances, a governmentally provided staff, and free mailing privileges, to name a few.[12] However, if the opportunity arose for legislators to pass additional measures favoring incumbents, they would be likely to do so.[13] Take the case of an elected representative who must be periodically reelected to remain in office, but is a member of a party that is in the minority in the legislature. The representative, in order to remain in office, must win the next election or be out of a job. The representative may believe that there is no better person for the job, and might wish to be reelected for what he perceives as the good of the electorate, or the representative may simply desire reelection for selfish reasons. Either way, the representative will have an incentive to favor measures that will enhance the probability of an incumbent being reelected.[14]

From the standpoint of the minority party, however, such measures would probably be viewed as undesirable, since the only possibility for a minority party to increase its strength in the legislature is to unseat incumbents from other parties. Since a majority is a valuable asset, a minority party has an interest in being able to unseat incumbents easily in order to strengthen its position. Each individual legislator has an incentive to remain in office, and so has an incentive to make it more difficult to unseat incumbents. The individual legislator, after all, would in all likelihood rather remain in the legislature as a member of a minority party than to increase the probability of not being reelected in order to strengthen the party's chances of gaining more seats. The incumbent member of a minority party would like to have more fellow party members elected, but would be more interested in retaining his own seat. This is the simple self-interest axiom of economics. As a result, all incumbents will be in favor of strengthening the ability of incumbents to be reelected.

In a very important sense, then, political competition is better characterized as competition between incumbents and nonincumbents than between parties. There is obvious political competition between parties, to be sure, but the less obvious coalition of incumbents against nonincumbents has important implications. The incumbents are the lawmakers, and have the incentive to pass rules in their favor, which is something nonincumbents will never be able to achieve. If a nonincumbent does beat an incumbent, then he leaves the coalition of nonincumbents to become an incumbent, and now has an incentive to continue the type of rulemaking that made it hard to get elected in the first place. In the contemporary United States, it is definitely more difficult for a nonincumbent to be elected than an incumbent, which means that part of the democratic aspect of legislator selection has been ended. In the sample noted earlier, incumbents defeated nonincumbents 85 percent of the time. If this figure were to be 100 percent, the system would be a democracy in name only. This issue will be discussed in more detail, and from a slightly different perspective, in Chapter 8.

Mark Crain has suggested that an important reason for the power of incumbents is the system of single-member legislative districts.[15] His basic argument rests upon an analogy between economic and political competition. If firms were to form a cartel, there would be the problem of enforcing the cartel agreement, since each individual member would have an incentive to cheat. One of the best ways is to divide the market geographically, assigning each firm an exclusive district over which the firm can exercise monopoly power. Another firm's sales in this exclusive district would be relatively easy to detect. The cartel is enforced by granting each firm an exclusive monopoly in an area, so that no firm directly competes with any other. Crain argues that this is in essence what happens with single-member legislative districts. The political market is divided geographically so that no incumbent ever competes directly with another incumbent.

Contrast this situation with a system of multimember districts. Take an example of a state that has five congressmen in the House of Representatives. Under the present single-member districting, each member would run against a nonincumbent for reelection, and no incumbent would ever directly compete with another incumbent. Under multimember districting the top five vote getters in the state would be elected, so all candidates would compete against one another. Under this situation, incumbents would be competing against other incumbents as well as any other challengers, so that there would no longer be the political cartel that exists in a single-member districting situation. Note that in the United States Senate, this same cartel situation arises even though there are two senators per state. Their terms are staggered so that an incumbent never has to run against another incumbent. Single-member districting may be the most significant factor in producing the cartel that has made it so difficult for challengers to unseat incumbents.

Representation with Multimember Districts

Under a system of multimember districts, more would change than just the ability of challengers to unseat incumbents. The character of the legislature would be different. Single-member districting will tend to elect a more homogeneous legislature than multimember districting. This conclusion is a direct implication of Downs's model of representative government.[16]

Under single-member districting there will be a tendency for the candidate most preferred by the median voter to be selected. The result will be a relatively homogeneous legislature consisting of median candidates. Under multimember districting, candidates will tend to be spread out over the distribution of voters. In a system where more than one candidate is elected from a district, if all candidates congregated at the median, as they would in the system where only one candidate per district is elected, then a candidate could represent voters at one end of the distribution and be elected. Although the candidate would not be able to get a majority of the votes, extreme candidates could get enough to be elected. Under multimember districting, winning candidates will tend to be spread evenly over the distribution of voters.

This can be demonstrated in Figure 7.3, which uses a Downsian model of political competition to illustrate the result of multimember districting. As described in chapter 2, single-member districts will elect a candidate with a platform representing the median voter, at M in Figure 7.3. If the two candidates collecting the largest number of votes were to be elected from the district, then a new party with platform P_1 could arise and win one seat. Political competition would then force the other parties to move their platforms to point P_2, away from the median. Political competition would then cause parties to offer platforms of either P_1 or P_2 in order to try to get elected. The exact location of P_1 and P_2 would depend upon how rapidly individual voter preferences changed as party platforms moved away from the median, so there would be no way to know exactly where P_1 and P_2 would be located without more information about voter preferences. In this sense the multimember district model is aesthetically less satisfying than the single-member district case, since with only this information the exact location of parties can be predicted in the single-member but not the multimember district case. One thing that can be demonstrated, though, is that in a two-member district, the parties will spread out over the political spectrum rather than congregate at the median.

The same logic would apply to three and more member districts. In a three-member district, the third member might squeeze in at M pushing P_1 and P_2 farther left and right, or might enter from one side pushing the party at that side to the median. The same process would apply to four-member districts. The larger the number of representatives elected from a district, the more diverse will be the platforms of the elected representatives.

When comparing single-member districts with multimember districts, there is more to be evaluated than simply the monopoly aspects of single-member districts. A system of single-member districts is likely to have a relatively homogeneous group of representatives, since the median voter will tend to be decisive in each district. Differences in representatives would be expected to be due only to differences in the preferences of the median voter across districts. Multimember districts, by contrast, would

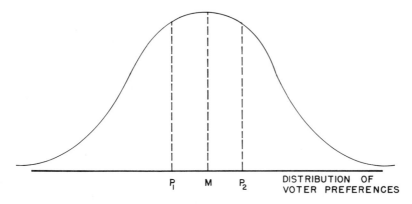

Fig. 7.3. Election of representatives in single-member and multi-member districts

be far more likely to elect candidates representing political platforms very different from the median. People with minority views would be more likely to be represented in the legislature, which tends to be viewed positively. On the negative side, however, elected representatives would hold far more diverse views, meaning that securing agreement among representatives would be more difficult. Within the context of the median voter model, the same voter would end up being represented in the final decisions of any legislature, assuming proportional representation, since the body of elected representatives would end up abiding by the views of the median representative.

Even though the same voter would end up being represented, actual legislative decisions might differ from one system to another. Under single-member districts, representatives have more monopoly power and would tend to pass more measures favoring the government and strengthening the ability to reelect incumbents. Under multimember districting, monopoly power of representatives would be smaller, but representatives would have a more difficult time reaching agreement. Different political decisions might result. The point of this section is to illustrate that the composition of the legislature and the nature of legislative decisions would be different under single-member when compared to multimember districts. Thus the simple observation of the monopoly power that arises from a system of single-member districts is not sufficient to imply that the system should be changed. In fact, where single-member districts already exist the question is probably irrelevant. Legislators will always favor single-member districts because the system enhances the legislator's power. Since the legal change from single-member to multimember districts would probably have to come from the legislature that is one change that has a very small probability of ever being considered.

Monopoly Bureaus and Economic Efficiency

Whenever the economic efficiency of institutional structures is examined, the allocation of resources through the competitive market is used as a benchmark to judge efficiency. Because of the desirable characteristics of the competitive outcome, there is a natural tendency to ascribe these same characteristics to the competitive process. This tendency may be—in part, anyway—what has prompted William Niskanen, after analyzing some causes of bureaucratic inefficiency, to recommend that bureaucracies be restructured to resemble competitive markets more closely.[17] However, when resources are allocated through a bureaucracy, the analog to a competitive market outcome is not necessarily most efficiently produced by an analog to the competitive market process.

This point was suggested by Earl Thompson.[18] after remarking on Niskanen's suggestion to increase the competitiveness of bureaus, Thompson said, "What an economist can profitably contribute to improving governmental efficiency are incentive systems which will induce more efficient behavior from our bureaucrats without requiring markets or elections." Although Niskanen's model of bureaucracy has had a large impact on the analysis of bureaucracy, there have been few (if any) suggestions for improvement of incentives along the lines suggested by Thompson. This section will work within the framework developed by Niskanen to suggest a simple institutional change that would cause the Niskanen-type bureau to produce at the analog to the competitive market outcome. Working within the Niskanen model, the conclusion will apply to Niskanen-type bureaucracies, but no sweeping claims of generality are being made. The section is included because it provides some surprising insights into property rights and incentive structures in the public sector.[19]

Property rights within a bureau are arranged in such a way that the bureaucrat is unable to capture any of the difference between the costs incurred and the benefits produced by the bureau. Thus, the bureaucrat will substitute other goals for profit maximization. Niskanen suggests that the goal of budget maximization will replace profit maximization in a bureaucracy, since many of the objectives of a bureaucrat (e.g., power, prestige, salary) are directly tied to the size of the bureau that the bureaucrat oversees. Niskanen also suggests that the bureau will be in a better bargaining position than its sponsor, since the bureaucrats have been information concerning the supply function of the bureau, and since the demand function of the sponsor is easily detected.

In addition, bureaus typically work for only one sponsoring organization, whereas sponsors typically oversee many bureaus. For these reasons, the bureau finds itself in a superior bargaining position, and is able to place its sponsor on its all-or-nothing demand curve.

The equilibrium conditions for a budget-maximizing bureaucracy that is able to place its sponsor on its all-or-nothing demand curve are shown in Figure 7.4. The bureau's marginal cost function is MC, and the sponsor's demand curve is D, making the sponsor's all-or-nothing demand curve DA. The bureau will maximize its budget by producing Q_B, and will extract the entire consumer surplus of the sponsor, so that triangle abc equals triangle cde. At margin, the cost of bureaucratic output exceeds its value by distance de.[20]

In examining the questions of resource allocation in a bureaucracy, a careful study of the supply and demand functions of the bureaucracy is revealing. The bureaucratic supply curve is the usual marginal cost curve resulting from input prices and a production function. Niskanen's demand constrained bureaucracy produces at the minimum total cost for each level of output, uses the most efficient scale of plant, and has the same marginal and average cost curves as an analogous firm in the market.

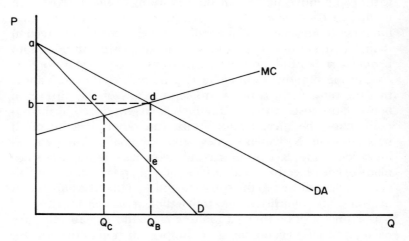

Fig. 7.4. Equilibrium for a budget-maximizing bureaucracy

There is nothing unique about the bureaucratic supply curve. The demand conditions faced by the bureaucracy differ from the usual market demand conditions, however, since the bureaucracy faces an all-or-nothing demand curve.

Given the demand and supply curves faced by a bureau, the constraints placed on bureaucrats cause them to produce an outcome which is identical to the result obtained in a competitive environment. Both bureaus and competitive firms are constrained to producing at minimum average cost. A competitive firm does so in order to maximize profits, whereas a bureau does so in order to maximize its budget. Both the bureau and the competitive firm earn no economic profits in equilibrium. Thus, the bureaucratically controlled market will exhibit the same type of equilibrium as the competitive market. Both produce at a point where supply equals demand; but whereas the Marshallian demand curve is the relevant demand curve for the market, the all-or-nothing demand curve is the relevant demand curve in a bureaucracy.

The all-or-nothing demand curve which is facing the bureaucracy is the curve to which the Marshallian market demand curve is marginal. Thus, in Figure 7.4, the bureau's supply curve is MC, the bureau's demand curve is DA, and the bureau's marginal revenue curve is D. As noted above, the constraints placed upon the bureau cause the bureau to produce where its supply curve intersects its demand curve, as a competitive industry would. If the bureau were profit maximizing rather than budget maximizing, it would attempt to produce at the point where its marginal revenue equals its marginal cost, implying an output of Q_c. Since the sponsor's demand curve is the bureau's marginal revenue curve, a profit maximizing monopolist would produce where MC equals D, which is the optimal level of output. Given the supply and demand curves faced by a bureau, a profit maximizing monopoly bureau will produce efficiently.

In contrast to the competitive solutions suggested by Niskanen, the analysis presented here suggests that a movement toward more monopolistic conditions would increase the efficiency of a bureaucracy. Specifically, allowing bureaus to maximize profits will yield economically efficient results. Although increased competition could also lead to economically efficient results, the monopoly institution might still have an advantage because it is not necessary to police a monopoly in order to get it to earn monopoly rents. There may be a significant cost involved in policing competition among government agencies, since there will be an incentive for them to collude.

This solution would still leave the purchasers of bureaucratic output on their all-or-nothing demand curves, however, albeit at the economically efficient level of output. Institutions could be devised that would transfer some of the surplus generated by the bureaucracy to the consumers. For example, positions in the bureaucracy could be auctioned to the highest bidder.[21] Although the details of this arrangement would have to be worked out, at least the monopolistic bureau leaves some surplus to be distributed. In the Niskanen-type bureaucracy, there is no surplus produced.

The profit maximizing monopolistic bureau might also successfully deal with a number of other problems that have been associated with bureaucratic supply. For example, Alchian has suggested that because bureaus are not privately owned, managers do not have an incentive to maximize the present value of the bureaucracy.[22] A profit maximizing monopoly bureau might solve this problem as well. But the purpose of this discussion is not to suggest a wholesale restructuring of bureaucracy. Rather it is to examine a particular institutional structure to discover an incentive system that would imply the efficient allocation of resources. Within the institutional structure implied in Niskanen's model of bureaucracy, monopoly appears superior to competition in producing an optimal allocation of resources.

This conclusion may not completely generalized to the real-world institutional structure of bureaucracy, but it does lend some insights. Perhaps auctioning monopoly rights and then allowing bureaus to maximize profits would be a viable alternative.[23] A more general implication, following Thompson's suggestion quoted at the beginning of this section, is that there may be innovative and unusual incentive systems that can be used to increase public sector efficiency. While this section certainly does not claim to have provided any definitive answers, it does suggest a possible avenue of inquiry.

Conclusion

In models of public sector activity, as in models of private sector activity, efficiency is generally the result of competition. But governments generally do not compete with one another, at least directly. Instead, political competition takes the form of competition for control of certain aspects of a monopoly government. Economists since Adam Smith have noted that producers in the private sector have an incentive to join together to monopolize markets, yet (possibly due to governmental controls over the private sector) the tendency toward monopoly appears to have greater momentum in the public sector. In the name of centralization and the elimination of duplication of effort, competing governmental agencies are consolidated.

The elements of monopoly in government have only been selectively sampled here, and some very important issues have not even been mentioned. For example, revenue sharing greatly contributes to monopoly government. The Federal government shares revenues with smaller governments under the condition that the smaller governments abide by Federal guidelines. The guidelines standardize the output of smaller governmental units, eliminating intergovernmental competition. The smaller governments have in effect formed a cartel under the umbrella of the Federal government, and are bribed to remain in the cartel by the revenue sharing grant. An overview of monopoly government could easily be the subject of another book rather than just a chapter, so this chapter will have to be considered merely illustrative.

The general topic of monopoly in government can be considered under two broad categories, though. The most obvious is the government bureaucracy that is the sole provider of many goods and services. Less obvious is the group of elected officials who do have to compete for office, but who find no competition for a specified period once they are elected, and find monopoly aspects in the election process as well. Tullock observed that under majority rule politics, only one majority can exist at a time, leading to the natural monopoly argument in political parties. Once elected, the winner-take-all nature of the majority rule system tends to reinforce those monopoly aspects. The next chapter looks at monopoly elements in government from a constitutional perspective, and so shines a slightly different light on the subject. The general conclusions, however, remain unchanged.

8

A Contractarian Model of the State

The preceding chapters have analyzed the political process primarily within a democratic framework, taking for granted the legitimacy of the democratic decision-making process in general. Some individuals are elected to public office, and the rest are assumed to have the right to vote. That right includes at least the right to elect the highest level of public officials, and sometimes includes the right to make collective decisions directly through referenda as well. This chapter will analyze the legitimacy of those political institutions that were earlier taken for granted.

The analysis put forth in this chapter is based upon the social contract theory of the state. This chapter deals with constitutional issues—those issues that determine "the rules of the game" within which members of the society interact—while previous chapters have examined the interaction of individuals within the bounds of constitutionally determined rules. While the analysis of this chapter works within the social contract theory of the state, it certainly does not accept that theory uncritically. To the contrary, this chapter works within the framework of the "new contractarians"[1] to develop a model that explains why the terms of the social contract can be expected to erode over time. The theory developed in this chapter is an explicitly dynamic theory that should serve to complement the earlier material in this book, and most of the contemporary literature on the economics of the public sector.[2]

Much of the recent economics literature has emphasized the growth of government bureaucracy and the inefficiency of public sector institutions. Some of this literature has consisted of empirical studies suggesting that output produced in the public sector is produced at greater cost than if it had been produced in the private sector.[3] These empirical studies have been supported by a wide variety of theoretical models which suggest that the institutional structure does not provide bureaucrats with the incentive to allocate resources efficiently.[4] Other studies have examined the political process and come to the conclusion that voters have an incentive to favor an inefficient allocation of resources.[5] Still other studies have alleged large welfare losses resulting from the competition for monopoly rents that can be produced by government restrictions of entry into some economic activities.[6] The central theme of all these studies is that big government tends to allocate resources inefficiently.

This type of research has grown relatively rapidly in the economics literature recently[7] and may reflect, in part anyway, the increasing proportion of economic resources that are allocated through the public sector. In both the United States and the United Kingdom, the public sector continues to command an increasing proportion of economic resources, and the trend shows no signs of abatement. Following the trend of the economy, the economics literature is devoting an increasing amount of attention to the allocation of economic resources through political processes.

Although many studies have examined, both theoretically and empirically, the economics of resources allocation through the public sector, this literature has done little to explain the relative increase in the size of the public sector.[8] This chapter will present a model that explains why a laissez-faire economy could be expected to evolve into an economy with greater and greater governmental influence over the allocation of resources.[9]

The problem to be analyzed in this chapter is a dynamic rather than a static one. The existing literature has done much to explain why there are incentives for government to be large. Explaining why the government is large is quite different from explaining why the government has grown, however. If the institutional environment is such that it creates large government, the question arises about why the government was not always so large. Since both the United States and the United Kingdom once had minimal governments, the phenomenon to be explained in these cases is not simply bigness, but growth.

To use an economic analogy, there are two quite distinct bodies of economic theory used to explain why prices are high as opposed to why prices are rising. Price theory explains that prices are at the levels they are due to, for examples, scarcity, the un-availability of substitutes, a less than competitive market structure, or government constraints on allowable trades. This theory of price can explain the existence of high prices in the same way that the current theory of bureaucracy can explain the existence of big government. The theory of price explains why prices are at their existing levels, but not why prices generally tend to rise. This second question about why there is inflation is explained with a different body of theory. Just as explaining why prices are at their current levels does not explain why prices continually rise, the existing bureaucracy theory that explains why government is big does not explain why government grows. The model in this chapter attempts to address this second question about the growth of government and thus attempts to explain a dynamic phenomenon of growth rather than a static phenomenon of size.[10]

The Continuing Social Contract

The central model behind the thesis of this chapter is built upon the foundation provided by some of the recent literature on the social contract theory of the state. The social contract theory of government can be traced to early beginnings—at least to the time of Locke and Rousseau[11]—and is a still-developing theory, as shown by the recent works by Buchanan and Rawls.[12] The basis of the social contract theory of government is that all individuals in a free society are bound in their interactions by an implicit social contract, which dictates the rights and responsibilities of the individuals within society. The individual need not take part in the writing of the constitution that governs his actions. All that is necessary is that he conceptually agree to the terms of the social contract.

One view of this conceptual agreement is presented by Buchanan and Tullock in *The Calculus of Consent*.[13] In that work, the distinction is emphasized between decision making at the constitutional level and decision making at the post-constitutional level. That distinction is a useful one for understanding the social contract theory of the state. In the social contract theory, conceptual agreement is necessary at the constitutional level of decision making. Individuals must agree on the rules that govern individual actions and interactions within society. Agreement is not necessary at the post-constitutional level. Many individuals might disapprove of the actions of some individual or group, but as long as that individual or group is acting within the provisions of the constitution, the social contract is being upheld. Indeed, the constitution could be expected to provide for many cases in which collective activities can be undertaken with less than unanimous approval, because the costs of arriving at a unanimous agreement are so high. The social contract theory only implies a conceptual unanimous agreement on the provisions of the constitution under which society operates.

A Theory of Justice by John Rawls suggests this same type of difference between the constitutional level of decision making and the post-constitutional level. Rawls suggests that the rules of society should be those rules which could be unanimously agreed upon by the individuals in society, assuming that this agreement takes place behind a "veil of ignorance," where no individual knows what position in society he will occupy after the rules are defined. That is, individuals must unanimously agree upon a constitution before they know their post-constitutional positions in society. Rawls's constitution, like that of Buchanan and Tullock, is the social contract to which there must be unanimous agreement among members of society.[14]

According to the social contract theory of the state, society can be viewed as a type of club, where all individuals conceptually agree to become members and adhere to the club rules. While there may not be general agreement about the desirability of any particular action taken by a club member or group of members, all members agree with the rules within which they must operate. In the case of an actual club, there is actual agreement among all club members regarding the club rules. Members volunteer to join the club, and the voluntary joining of the club signifies a voluntary agreement with the constitution of the club. Anyone who does not agree with the rules of the club need not join. In society, this is not the case. Individuals are born into society whether they like it or not; and once there, they must adhere to the rules of the existing social contract. They are not free to join or not to join. Here, the social contract theory of the state must fall back upon the conceptual agreement of all members of society. The state operates as if all members of society had agreed to its rules—as if there is unanimous approval of the constitution.[15]

This requirement of conceptual unanimous approval of the constitutional rules is probably the weakest link in the social contract theory of the state, since in most cases, few if any of the existing members of society have participated in the writing and approving of the constitutional rules which govern society. But before the social contract theory of the state can claim to be a valid model of reality, the theory must explain how all members of society may be considered in conceptual agreement with the constitutional rules by which they are governed.

James Buchanan provides one answer to this problem in *The Limits of Liberty*. Buchanan begins with the concept of an "anarchistic equilibrium" that would exist in the absence of any type of social contract defining the rules under which individuals interact. In this state of anarchy, no individual would recognize any rights of other individuals. Implied in this anarchistic equilibrium is some "natural distribution" of income which would accrue to individuals under this social structure. In this situation, all individuals could be made better off by agreeing to write some social contract binding each individual in society to follow certain rules in his interactions with his fellow man, and in turn granting each individual certain rights. Each individual, finding it in his own self-interest to agree to the terms of the social contract, would agree to abide by the terms of the contract. All individuals would enjoy increased welfare in moving from anarchy into the society governed by the social contract.

As was already noted, most individuals in any present society did not actually agree to be bound by the terms of the existing constitutional rules. But the conceptual agreement with the terms of the constitution is described in the following manner in Buchanan's model. At every point in time, individuals can visualize the natural distribution that would exist in society in an anarchistic equilibrium. From this point, they might imagine how they would expect to fare in a writing of a new social contract, beginning from this natural distribution that would exist in anarchy. If an individual feels that he could not expect to be much better off under a new social contract, then he realizes that the existing social contract is about as good from his standpoint as any that might reasonably expect to take the existing contract's place. Therefore, he is in conceptual agreement with the existing social contract.

The concept of rewriting the social contract from a condition of anarchistic equilibrium places bounds on the limits to which the existing contract can abuse the liberty of the members of society. If disenchantment with the existing social contract becomes generalized, then some type of revolution will result, and a new social contract will be written from the conceptual origin of the natural distribution. Thus, those who are presently in political power should continually be adjusting the terms of the social contract to reflect changes in the underlying natural distribution. By so doing, they will always be able to satisfy this condition of conceptual agreement with the social contract. If they are not sensitive to the underlying natural distribution, then there should be a general uprising to attempt to write a new social contract.

Buchanan does not suggest that the conditions necessary for the social contract to exist are always met. Indeed, it is possible for those in power to coerce others into a position far worse than would exist under a conceptual social contract. But to do so would require coercion and oppression by the rulers of society: the society would not be a group of free individuals. Rather, the social contract theory would apply in a situation where individuals are free, but work within the constitutional framework to advance their personal well-being, rather than trying to write a new social contract. In this latter type of system, conceptual agreement with the social contract exists, and the social contract model of the state is applicable. In such a society, there is a continuing social contract, where all members of society are in continual conceptual agreement with the existing constitutional rules.

The concept of the continuing social contract is graphically depicted in the two-person example shown in Figure 8.1. The horizontal axis measures the utility of individual X, and the vertical axis measures the utility of individual Y. The natural distribution would provide the two individuals with the level of utility indicated by point A. Under a mutually agreeable social contract, both individuals would expect to be substantially better off than

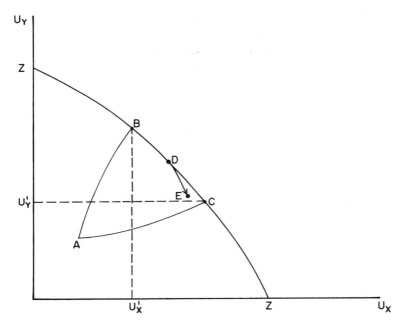

Fig. 8.1. The continuing social contract

they would be in anarchy. For example, individual X would figure that he could do no worse than utility level U', and individual Y would figure that he could do no worse than utility level U'. Thus, where ZZ is the utility possibilities frontier, the social contract could be expected to emerge that would yield utility levels represented by some point between B and C on the frontier.

The Emergence of the Contract

None of the above discussion implies that the social contract will be based on laissez-faire or classical liberal principles. Buchanan emphasizes that the social contract theory only describes the principles by which a legitimate social contract can emerge and says nothing about the terms of the contract.[16] Rawls takes his theory a bit farther and describes what terms he would expect to see emerge,[17] but his contractarian model does not necessarily imply that his postulated terms of the contract would in fact be the actual terms to emerge. In short, the social contract theory says nothing about the terms or conditions of the resulting contract.

This analysis has nothing to add to that aspect of the social contract theory. The model presented here simply assumes that a contract based on classical liberal principles will emerge within the framework presented above. In such a society, the role of government would be minimal—perhaps limited only to enforcing contracts and protecting property rights. The model will be developed by assuming the most favorable circumstances for the contractarian emergence of a liberal society.

Within the framework of Figure 8.1, a free society could be thought of as emerging in the following manner. All individuals would picture themselves in the situation of anarchistic equilibrium and imagine a social contract developing from the natural distribution at point A. The constitution might be written in such a manner that individuals would largely be behind a Rawlsian veil of ignorance, at least with respect to some issues. For example, individual X might be thought of as a person who, in his new role in society, will be an administrator in the government that is described in the social contract. Individual Y, on the other hand, will continue in some private sector role within society. The social contract could be written in such a way that at the time of the writing of the contract, no individual would know whether he would be selected to serve in the government or whether he would remain in the private sector. Thus the veil of ignorance would be set up within the domain of the contract, and the individuals behind the veil could be expected to pick a social contract yielding utility levels somewhere close to the middle of points B and C, such as point D. Individuals would pick a point such as D because they would not know at the time of the writing of the social contract whether they will be individual X or individual Y.

This process is a close theoretical analog to the writing of the American constitution, since that constitution was written to embody classical liberal principles, and since at the time of the writing of the constitution, individuals did not know whether they would be elected to serve in the government. Therefore, individuals who later became officials within the government actually were operating behind a veil of ignorance at the time of the writing of the constitution—at least with respect to whether they would have a position in the government. For this reason, the social contract model seems to have a bit more than just conceptual correspondence with the American case.[18]

After the writing of the social contract, the veil of ignorance is lifted, and individuals take their places within society. Some individuals take roles within the government, such as individual X, while others find themselves outside the government, such as individual Y. Initially, the constitution should provide safeguards against the potential for individuals within the government to abuse their power. These safeguards would have been designed at the constitutional level in order to protect and maintain the liberal society.

A problem is likely to arise, however, due to the fact that a constitution written to guide a society that endures through time must be flexible enough to allow for changes, so that the terms of the constitution can adapt to new and unforeseen circumstances that will arise in the society. This is a problem because people outside the government are, by definition, outside the process that will modify the terms of the social contract, so that any changes that will occur must be initiated by the government. Modifications to the social contract are not made behind the veil of ignorance and are likely to be made in favor of those who have the power to make the change. Over time, then, the people in the government will have an incentive to improve their position by giving themselves more and more power, and the liberal principles of the society will be eroded.

Within the framework of Figure 8.1, those individuals such as X, who are in the government, will find it in their interest to redefine the social contract in order to move the outcome toward C. In the process, there could be some inefficiency, so that the actual altered social contract locates society somewhat inside the utility possibilities frontier, at a position such as E.[19] The point is that X will have an incentive to sacrifice some of the benefits accruing to Y in order to increase his own benefits.

It is true that the conceptual rewriting of the contract from the starting point of A will provide limits to how far the liberal constitution can be eroded before the individuals in society will have to be coerced into accepting the existing conditions. In order to maintain freedom, the government might want to observe the limit on individual Y's utility set by U_y. But staying within these limits is something different from continually drawing up a new and mutually acceptable social contract. The existing social contract will always be biased in favor of those who hold governmental power, since they are the ones who have the ultimate power of altering the terms of the existing constitution.

Individuals outside the government have the incentive to see that this bias is alleviated; however, the mechanism of change comes from within the government. That is, individuals outside the government must follow the rules set forth in the social contract in order to become a member of the government, and only then is the mechanism of change available for their use. But once individuals become a part of the government, they are no longer in the position of individual Y, but of individual X. They are now the ones who are favored by the social contract, and they have no incentive to alter the bias.

Changes in the Contract over Time

The potential for this type of erosion of the principles of the social contract could be expected to increase over time. As a practical matter, a system of checks and balances designed from behind the veil of ignorance probably could be eroded only slowly. Additionally, individuals have the potential to be voted out of office, so that when in the position of individual X they award themselves benefits, they may in the next term find themselves in the position of individual Y. Thus, as incumbents find more ways of keeping themselves in office, the likelihood of erosion of the terms of the contract will increase.

There may be a more important reason for the terms of the contract to erode over time, however. In a lesser developed economy, where the actual starting point for negotiation of the contract is close to anarchy, individuals would probably have a chance of surviving independently of other individuals in the society. Every member of the society would be largely self-sufficient. The writing of a contract would confer benefits, of course, as shown in the model in Figure 8.1, but the benefits would be largely due to the fact that when property is protected, there is the potential for capital accumulation.

After a society operates under the social contract for a period of time, this will have two effects upon the model developed in Figure 8.1. First, due to the increased productivity and greater capital stock of society, the well-being of its members will be enhanced. Within the framework of this model, that will shift the utility possibilities frontier outward from ZZ to Z'Z' in Figure 8.2. Second, the society will become more interdependent, so that in a condition of anarchy the prospects for each member of the society would not be as good as if the society were not presently as interdependent. For example, the typical individual at the time of the American Revolution, when the society was less interdependent, would probably have better prospects under anarchy than the typical individual today. Within the framework of this model, that would shift the point of anarchistic equilibrium back from point A to point F. Thus, as an economy develops, the utility possibilities frontier shifts out, and at the same time the natural distribution of income moves closer to the origin. Both of these changes occur due to the fact that the social contract has allowed the society to develop.

Figure 8.2 shows that both of these factors will increase the range within which a renegotiated social contract would be expected to fall. Given the bias that was explained earlier, as time goes on the terms of the contract would continually be moving toward point H, farther from point G. As Figure 8.2 shows, it is possible for both individuals to have a higher lower bound on their expected utility in a renegotiation immediately after the writing of the contract than after society has developed under the protection of the social contract. For individual Y, U' is greater than U''. As a society develops under the social contract, that development alone increases the potential for an erosion of the terms of the contract.[20] Thus, the model developed here would predict that a society that is founded upon classical liberal principles would be expected to see those principles eroded over time.

There is one aspect of the evolving social contract over time that alters somewhat the characteristics of interdependence over time. As a society becomes more complex and the utility possibilities frontier shifts outward, each individual finds himself more dependent upon the social structure in which he lives. Yet, as the individual's dependence upon the society in general increases, dependence upon every specific member of the society decreases.

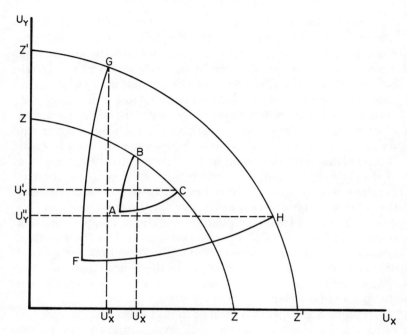

Fig. 8.2. Changes in the contract over time

Individuals in a more complex and interdependent society rely less on particular individuals, but more on the society in general for their well-being. This heavier reliance on the society, even as individuals become more independent from other individuals, is what causes the liberal principles of a society to have the potential for erosion over time.[21]

Practical Problems

No easy solutions suggest themselves for the problem of the erosion of the social contract over time. The constitution may be written in such a way as to try to minimize the ability of those in power to alter it in their favor, but any time some mechanism for change exists within the constitution, this mechanism is also a potential mechanism for abuse by those in power. And a constitution with no flexibility to deal with change would certainly be destined to a short life. The constitution of the United States has stood up reasonably well for about 200 years, but the abuses of power are beginning to show, as the society moves farther from liberty, and closer to Leviathan. The system of checks and balances still checks and balances, but the whole system has grown to almost unmanageable proportions. This is not to say that a system of checks and balances is not the best safeguard. It may well be.

Another method of inhibiting the abuse of the constitution, but one that is seldom viewed in this light, is democracy. There is an increasing tendency of people to think—and this is especially true of contemporary Americans—that democracies use a system of majority rule in order to carry out the will of the majority. In some cases this may be true, but in the American case in particular, it was not the intent of the framers of the constitution to devise a system that would cater to the will of the majority. Rather, the American constitution was designed in order to protect the rights of the individual, and to allow individuals to be free from the coercion of their fellows, and of their government. Majority rule is simply a system of selecting those who will occupy governmental positions, and safeguard the individual rights that are guaranteed in the constitution. The basis of the American form of government is the protection of individual rights, not the furthering of the will of the majority.

Seen within the framework of the model presented in this chapter, the function of majority rule should become clear. The postconstitutional danger involved in writing a social contract is that those who have the power of government are in a position to alter the constitution in a manner that will benefit them. The provision of elected representatives operating the government provides some safeguard that the individuals who are now in the government will not always be in the government. Thus, during their tenure in office, they will be less likely to abuse the constitution in such a manner that damages the interests of those outside the government, since they someday will be outside the government themselves. The system of majority rule in the election of representatives is a mechanism of rotating the individuals who have government power. Individuals who abuse the constitution will not be reelected.

Recognition of this safeguard can most clearly be seen in the case of the president. For over a century, presidents recognized the value of rotating the holder of the office, and began the precedent of holding the office for only two terms. When this precedent was not followed, Congress enacted it into law. The other two branches illustrate the abuse of this safeguard. The courts, above any other branch of government, threaten to take over much power initially delegated to other government agents. Only the judges do not have to be reelected. Similarly, more and more political advantages are being given to Congress, so that an incumbent will be reelected almost every time. As being a congressman becomes more and more a lifetime profession, the Congress can be expected to abuse the constitution in its favor to an increasing degree. The constitutional safeguard of democracy is being eroded when individuals are able to be legislators as a lifelong occupation. Perhaps the best solution would be to limit the terms of legislators to a finite period in the same manner that the term of the president of the United States is limited.

The argument presented here certainly does not irreparably damage the theory of the continuing social contract, but it does raise a troublesome point with respect to the continuing nature of the contract. The weakest link in the social contract theory of the state is probably the requirement that all members must conceptually be in agreement with the contract. Buchanan has addressed this problem by using the concept of an anarchistic equilibrium, and allowing all men to compare the terms of the existing contract with the terms of a new social contract that might be written from the starting point of anarchy. If the existing contract falls within the limits of the terms that might reasonably be expected to emerge under a new contract, then the members of society can be thought of as being in conceptual agreement with the terms of the existing contract.

The argument in this chapter does not dispute the model of conceptual agreement used by Buchanan, but it does suggest that the conceptual agreement with the terms of the existing social contract is not equivalent to a continual rewriting of the contract. The limits within which reasonable men might expect the terms of a new social contract to fall might be rather broad, and are probably becoming more and more broad as individuals within society are becoming more dependent upon cooperation with each other. This argument suggests that within these broad limits, a continuing social contract should be expected to be biased in favor of the individuals within the government, and that the continuing contract should become more biased over time as the constitutional limits placed upon governmental officials are slowly eroded. There may be mechanisms that will help to slow this erosion; but ultimately, those who do not command governmental power will find themselves at the lower limits of their expectations of terms for a new social contract.

On a more practical level, the argument presented in this chapter is discouraging for those who would hope to move the American (or British) society back toward the liberal principles that guided it a century ago. The eroded liberal constitutional provisions that once governed the country are not likely to be restored by working within the framework of the existing social contract since the existing contract offers larger benefits to those within the government than they would receive under a return to liberalism. If the existing contract contains some inefficiency in the economic sense, it is conceptually possible that a Pareto superior move could be found in which those within the present government could be compensated in exchange for the writing of a new contract. Practically, such a Pareto superior move would be difficult to make, since the benefits that governors now expect to receive from the status quo will accur over time, and society may not be wealthy enough to pay immediate compensation. The present government would be reluctant to accept an agreement for future compensation, since once a new form of government took power, it might find a mechanism for reducing or eliminating continued compensation to the old government.

The continuing social contract theory of the state has a great deal of appeal, both as a theory of the ideal mechanism for governing people according to their desires, and as a descriptive theory of governmental activity in free societies. It appears, however, that there is some divergence between the nature of a continuing social contract, and an ideal social contract that is being continually renegotiated.

Conclusion

The purpose of this chapter is to use the contractarian framework to explain why a society based on laissez-faire principles would be expected to have an increasing amount of governmental activity over time. The economics literature has paralleled the development of the British and American economies by devoting more of its attention to resource allocation through the public sector. The model developed here explains why that development would be likely to occur.

Immediately after the writing of the social contract, the range within which renegotiation would be expected to occur would be relatively narrow, forcing those in power to adhere closely to the terms of the contract or lose their power. As the society develops under the protection of the contract, the bounds of expected renegotiation would continue to widen, leaving those in power a wider margin within which to exercise that power and still be able to retain it. With increased development and interdependence comes an increased potential for erosion of the original terms of the contract.

We hope this model will, at least partially, fill a gap in the economics literature. The literature discusses in detail the operation of a laissez-faire economy and is developing an equally detailed theory of resource allocation through the public sector. This chapter links these two bodies of literature by explaining how a laissez-faire economy could be expected to evolve toward one with increasing governmental activity.

Economic Efficiency and the Evolution of the Common Law

Much of the material in this book has been devoted to discussing problems associated with growth in government. This discussion has primarily focused on the incentives for and methods whereby the government commands a larger portion of economic resources than would be optimal. In the past two chapters, a different, albeit related, problem of growth in government has been introduced: the growth over time of the power of the government to legislate change. Growth in the government's command over resources and growth in the government's power of legislation are certainly closely related, and casual observation certainly suggests that those nations which, politically, are relatively free of government regulation and control over the lives of their citizens are also the nations which have relatively small public sectors in economic terms. Economic growth in government has, likewise, brought with it an increase in the government's control over its citizens.[1] The purpose here is not to discuss these trends, but to focus instead on the development of law—the rules by which society operates.

New law can be developed in two ways. Legislatures may pass statutes declaring a general rule that will be applicable to all cases which meet certain conditions, or courts may make a ruling in the outcome of a specific case which will be used as a precedent in determining the outcome of similar future cases. This first type of law is called statutory law, while the latter is common law. Statutory law is also subject to court interpretation, which blurs this categorization somewhat, but courts have traditionally tried to adhere to the letter of the law in interpreting statutes, whereas they are not so bound in developing common law. The development of laws that enhance the power of the government, as discussed in the last two chapters, has been a development of statutory law. The basic premise set forth in those chapters is that the government has an incentive to pass laws that favor those in the government. This chapter will discuss the common law, which is the alternative to statutory law.

Arguments could be made that statutory law will be more efficient in some circumstances and common law in others. The present analysis does not dispute that, but it is interesting to note in this context that the democratic government of ancient Greece had executive and judicial branches of government, but had no lesislature. Judges were elected for limited terms to adjudicate disputes, and the law developed in a manner very similar to the common law system in operation today.[2] This strongly suggests that it would be possible today to substitute common law for some areas of statutory law, especially considering the motives for some legislation. This background provides an introduction to an analysis of the common law.

Common and Statutory Law

Economic analysis of law has usually placed common and statutory law in the same category, since both types of law compose the rules which specify the rights and obligations of individuals within a society.[3] When analyzing the effect of a specific law under specific conditions, this approach is well justified. Frequently, however, the law must be applied to new and unforeseen circumstances. In these cases, there may be important differences between the operation of statutory and common law. Statutory law has no intrinsic corrective mechanism that guides it toward efficient decisions. In contrast, the system of precedent which is inherent in the common law provides a self-adjusting mechanism which guides the common law, as if by an "invisible hand," to serve the best interest of society.

Statutory law conforms to the economist's traditional notion about the law. The legislature has decided upon a set of well-defined rules under which a society shall operate. These rules are listed in a legal code, and when a legal question arises, it is resolved by applying the appropriate statute. The common law is, by contrast, not written down as a set of rules,[4] but rather is implied in past court decisions which will be used as precedents in future cases. Statutory law, simply because it is written down as the legislature's opinion of the law that will produce a desirable outcome under a general set of circumstances, is inflexible in adapting to new and unforeseen circumstances. Statutory law is flexible only to the (sometimes considerable) extent that the wording is subject to interpretation. Common law, on the other hand, is not bound by a specific wording of the law, but relies on judicial interpretation of general legal concepts implied in past court decisions. This chapter will draw upon some examples in the development of the tort of negligence, but the emphasis is not on certain efficient outcomes that have arisen in the common law. Rather, this chapter emphasizes the efficiency of the process through which the common law develops.

Lawyers have long recognized that the adversary process used in court cases generates, in addition to a decision in the particular case being tried, a legal precedent that may be applied to similar future cases.[5] In the development of the common law, the actual law that applies to a particular case is not written down in any one place, but is implied in past court decisions involving similar circumstances. A possible objection to the system of common law would be that if the law were instead written down as a specific set of statutes, the law would be less ambiguous. This objection is not of practical importance, since in the vast majority of common law cases, the applicable law is not in the least ambiguous, and most cases are, therefore, settled out of court. In addition, the application of a general statute to a particular set of circumstances is also frequently the course of a legitimate legal dispute. There is no reason to believe that a general statute, when applied to the unique facts of a specific case, will be any less ambiguous than applying legal precedents developed in similar previous cases.

There is some reason to believe that the process through which the common law develops is a more efficient lawmaking device, in the sense that it is more likely to construct the law in such a manner that the intended consequences of law are its actual consequences. For this reason, the common law is more likely to embody efficient economic incentives than is statutory law. The efficiency of the common law is due to the manner in which legal precedent is used in deciding the outcomes of specific cases, and can be attributed to two characteristics in the use of precedent and the development of the law on a case-by-case basis. First, it is easier to decide what an efficient outcome is in a specific case than it is to construct an efficient general rule; and second, the process of broadening and narrowing precedents acts as an "invisible hand" that guides the common law toward the most efficient social rules.

The Invisible Hand in the System of Precedent

The first advantage possessed by the system of precedent—that the law is decided on a case-by-case basis—assists in developing efficient law because constructing a general rule to apply to a broad category of cases is more difficult, and could not possibly take account of the infinite variety of possible circumstances, than deciding what an efficient rule would be in a specific case. The following section will describe some court cases involving negligence, so a hypothetical and clear-cut example will be employed here as a prelude to the next section. Assume that, while building an addition to his house, your neighbor has left some boards with exposed nails in them lying on the sidewalk by his house overnight. You are walking along the dark sidewalk and trip on the boards, injuring yourself on the exposed nails. Your neighbor was clearly negligent and would be legally liable for your injury. In the unlikely event that this case was not settled out of court, the court would undoubtedly find your neighbor guilty of the tort of negligence, and would order your neighbor to compensate you for your injury.

Assume that this is the first case of its type, and the judge decides to award you damages based upon your neighbor's negligence. A precedent has been established in the case which implies that when one individual is injured due to the negligence of another, the negligent individual is held liable for the damages that would have been avoided in the absence of his negligence. While this general rule of negligence seems to be operating in this particular case, the court will not state the rule as a general rule. Rather, it will state that in this particular case, with all of its particular circumstances, your neighbor is guilty of negligence and is, therefore, liable for damages resulting from his negligence. In future cases which use this case as a precedent, it will be up to the injured party to prove that the particular circumstances in a new case make the case conform to the general category of cases toward which the rule of negligence ought to apply. After many similar court cases in which the rule of negligence was judged to apply, the rule would become firmly established as a part of the common law.

Note that in this particular hypothetical case the court decision implies a rule that provides an incentive for individuals to avoid negligent behavior, which is economically efficient. The implied rule that an individual will be liable for damages caused by his negligent behavior gives individuals the incentive to avoid careless behavior that might injure another individual, as long as the cost of being careful is less than the expected damage done to others as a result of carelessness.[6] This efficient rule could have been enacted as a statute, rather than evolving via common law. A statute stating that "When one party is injured as a result of the negligent behavior of another, the negligent party is liable for the damages done to the injured party" would have produced the same decision in the above case. In this particular instance, there would be no difference between a statutory rule and a common law rule.[7] The important difference, and the reason why making law on a case-by-case basis has an advantage over the construction of a general rule, is that there may be some presently unforeseen circumstances that might arise in which the application of the general rule would provide inefficient rather than efficient incentives. Indeed, in the example just given, there will be some cases when it would provide inefficient incentives to hold a negligent party liable for damages done due to the party's negligence. Some examples will be given in the next section. The problem in formulating a general rule of negligence (or anything else) is that all of the desirable exceptions and qualifications to the general rule cannot be foreseen in a complex world, and the following of a specific wording of a general rule would sometimes result in the establishment of clearly inefficient law.

The making of law on a case-by-case basis does not imply that the law is vague or arbitrary. In almost every case, there is a clearly established precedent which will unambiguously apply. Only when the law must be applied to new and unforeseen circumstances will the courts be in a position to establish a new precedent. At these times, it is desirable to make a decision based on the new case rather than to apply the wording of a statute that did not foresee the circumstances of the particular case. Here, the flexibility of common law gives it a tremendous advantage in producing efficient incentives.

In the example above, the rule implying efficient incentives was used to decide the case; but the possibility always exists that a well-meaning judge or legislature could inadvertently decide a case or pass a law that implied inefficient incentives.[8] In the case of statutory law, there is no mechanism by which the law will tend to be corrected. The law could only be repealed by the legislature, and that would rarely occur. In the common law, on the other hand, the process of broadening and narrowing precedent tends to guide the common law toward more efficient social rules. This is probably the most important characteristic in causing the efficient development of the common law.

Assume that in the above example of the negligent builder the case had been decided in favor of your neighbor, who was not held liable for your injuries. Then another case arises in which an individual has dug a ditch across the sidewalk to install some plumbing and has not covered or marked the ditch at night. His neighbor walks down the dark sidewalk and is injured by falling into the ditch. If the first case were decided on the basis of an inefficient statute absolving negligent parties from being liable for the results of their negligence, the courts would be bound on the basis of the statute to absolve the ditchdigger of liability also. Since negligence would be less costly, there would be an increase of negligent behavior and of injuries due to negligence. But since the first case was incorrectly decided on the basis of common law court decision, not a statute, the precedent would be likely to be narrowed to exclude the present case. The court could rule that although there was some similarity in the cases, the original court decision was meant only to apply to cases where pedestrians fell on nail-studded boards at night on Oak Street, and does not apply to pedestrians falling into ditches on Maple Street.[9] Thus, the precedent does not apply, and the ditchdigger is held liable for damages due to his negligence. The precedent of the incorrectly decided case would be narrowed until it could not be used, and the initial error in the development of the common law would be rectified.

If the original case were correctly decided, as originally hypothesized, then it would have been used as precedent in the case of the negligent ditchdigger, and the precedent would have been broadened. After several cases have been decided upon the rule of negligence, negligence would clearly be established as a tort under the law. In order for the law to develop efficiently in this manner, judges must merely be able to recognize that a particular application of the law would lead to efficient (or inefficient) results. If judges are usually able to recognize efficient outcomes in specific cases, then an efficient set of common law rules will tend to emerge from the process through which common law is produced. The mechanism of broadening and narrowing precedent is the invisible hand of the common law. That feature of the common law allows the *tâtonnement* of the common law toward an efficient outcome, just as the competitive market allows the groping of the economy toward efficiency.

One suggestion of this section is that the process through which the common law develops includes a system of precedent which guides the law toward efficient legal outcomes in a manner similar to the way in which competition guides the economy toward efficient outcomes. Another suggestion of this section is that the situations toward which laws must apply are complex and unpredictable—a suggestion that might well be demonstrated by example. The next section of this chapter will examine a few cases in the development of the tort of negligence, focusing on the way in which efficient incentives are incorporated into the law on a case-by-case basis in order to account for circumstances that would not easily be foreseen. The negligence cases presented are those which have established precedents that were broadened and strengthened within the law. The examples are intended to illuminate the two points described in this section: that the common law does have a mechanism for producing efficient decisions, and that the development of the law on a case-by-case basis is more likely to produce efficient law than the construction of inflexible general rules.

The Evolution of the Rule of Negligence[10]

Recognition in the courts of negligence as a distinct tort for which one might be held liable began in the early part of the nineteenth century.[11] For purposes of illustration, the basic foundation of the negligence rule could be thought of as stated in the previous section: when one party is injured as the result of the negligent behavior of another, the negligent party is liable for damages done to the injured party. This rule implied efficient incentives when applied to the two hypothetical cases discussed earlier and could be regarded as the plaintiff's basis for bringing suit in the case of *Butterfield v. Forrester*.[12] In this case, Forrester was making repairs on his house, and in the process had placed a pole part way across a road, partially obstructing the road. Near dusk, but when there was still enough light to see the pole at a distance of 100 yards, Butterfield was violently riding his horse down the same road. Butterfield ran into the pole extended from Forrester's house, injuring himself, and brought suit against Forrester on the basis that Forrester was negligent in having obstructed the roadway with the pole. According to the simple rule of negligence just articulated, Forrester would be liable; however, the court did not rule that way in this case. The court reasoned that although Forrester had negligently placed the pole across the road, Butterfield should have seen the pole if he had been exercising ordinary care and, therefore, should have been able to avoid the injury.

The decision in this case clearly deviates from the simple notion of negligence upon which the hypothetical cases in the previous section were based, but for a good reason. The decision in this case implies that even if an individual is negligent in an instance, another individual must use ordinary care in order to avoid injuries due to the negligence. If individuals such as Butterfield were to be compensated for their injuries, the law would provide no incentive for them to avoid injury due to the negligence of another. The principle used in this case is known as contributory negligence, and does not replace the earlier articulated notion of negligence, but complements it. Forrester would still be held liable for any damages to others as a result of his negligence, if other individuals were exercising ordinary care. The incentive to avoid negligent behavior is retained. But individuals who could have avoided injury by simply exercising ordinary care will not be compensated, which provides an incentive for individuals to avoid injury to themselves when others are negligent. By holding Butterfield to be contributorily negligent, the court established efficient incentives for both potential negligent individuals and potential victims of negligence.[13] The precedent in the *Butterfield* case has been broadened, and now is firmly established as a part of the common law. If the decision had been incorrect, the precedent probably would have been narrowed in later cases where judges recognized the poor incentives implied in the decision.

The case of *Davies v. Mann*[14] draws upon the concepts of negligence and contributory negligence, but demonstrates that these concepts alone do not provide a proper incentive in all cases. In this case, Davies owned a donkey which he had left to graze in a public road, and had fettered the donkey's forefeet so that it could not wander away. A wagon pulled by a team of three horses, owned by Mann and driven by a servant of Mann, was riding down the road. The wagon struck and killed the donkey, and Davies brought suit to recover damages. The defense used by Mann was that the donkey was illegally in the road, and furthermore, that if the donkey's forefeet were not fettered it could have moved out of the way of the wagon. Therefore, Davies was contributorily negligent, and should not collect damages. The court ruled that even if Davies was contributorily negligent, the driver of the wagon still had the last clear chance to avoid the accident. Because he did not exercise his last clear chance, he should be liable for damages due to his negligence. Again, the law has been extended to fit a new circumstance not foreseen by the contributory negligence doctrine: if an individual has the last clear chance to avoid an accident and fails to exercise it, he is liable for damages. This case illustrates another example where the law provides an efficient incentive in a new circumstance. Even though an individual has exposed himself to a potential injury due to his own negligence, others still have the incentive to avoid injuring the negligent individual.

The simple rule of negligence first articulated has been extended by the precedents set in the past two cases to include the corollary doctrines of contributory negligence and last clear chance. Even with these two corollaries, a situation might still arise in which the modified rule of negligence did not imply efficient incentives, as demonstrated by *British Columbia Electric Ry*.

Co. v. Loach.[15] In this case, Benjamin Sands and another man were riding a loaded horse-drawn wagon across a railroad crossing, and neither man noticed that a train was coming until it was too late for them to get out of the way of the train. The driver of the train was first able to see the wagon when he was 400 feet from the crossing. Ordinarily, the train should have been able to stop in 300 feet, but the train had left that morning with a defective brake, and so was unable to stop in time to avoid a collision. The train hit the wagon, killing Sands, and Loach brought the original suit to collect damages for the estate of Sands. Under the negligence rule, described at the beginning of the paragraph, the railway company had a strong case. The railway company was negligent for having a defective brake, but Sands was contributorily negligent for not looking to see that the train was approaching. The railway company was absolved of liability under the contributory negligence doctrine; and due to the defective brake, the railway company did not have the last clear chance. Nevertheless, the court ruled in favor of Loach, noting that although the railway did not actually have the last clear chance in this case, it should have had the last clear chance if its equipment had not been defective. This decision implied a constructive last clear chance rule, stating that if an individual should have had the last clear chance to avoid an accident, but due to his own negligence he did not have the last clear chance, then he would still be liable for damage that could have been avoided if he had been able to exercise his last clear chance. Once again the court has provided an efficient incentive to avoid injury due to negligence. Individuals must not negligently give up the last clear chance, or they will be liable for damages due to their negligence.

The doctrine of negligence that has just been described demonstrates the ability of the common law to evolve in a manner that creates efficient incentives in a difficult matter that probably could not be effectively done by statute. The problem involved in creating an effective negligence rule is that efficient incentives at the margin imply that all individuals in an accident have an incentive to avoid all damage at the margin. Thus, all individuals should be liable for the full marginal damage of an accident. At the same time, the sum of the total liabilities of all individuals should equal the total damage in order to produce the optimal incentive to prevent accidents. The proper marginal incentives could be generated by making every individual who is party to an accident liable for the total damage done in the accident. Each individual would then always be able to benefit by the full amount of any marginal damage that he could avoid. At the point in time where the accident was inevitably going to occur, the proper marginal incentives would exist, but the resulting total liability of all parties to the accident would be the amount of the damages multiplied by the number of participants in the accident. The result of holding each party liable for the total damages is that the expected loss to all parties to the accident is larger than the actual damages, and would result in an overinvestment in accident prevention. The marginal incentives would be correct, but the total incentive to avoid accidents would be too great. Under an alternative rule where the damages are divided among the parties, the total incentives would be correct, but the marginal incentive to avoid damage would be too low.

The doctrine of negligence developed by the courts produced the correct incentives both in total and at the margin. The total incentive for accident prevention is correct because the total liability of all parties is equal to the amount of damage done. The marginal incentives are also correct due to the intricate way in which the assignment of liability is determined. As the sequence of events that leads to an accident occurs, an individual at each step of that sequence will be held liable for the total damages done due to his negligence, if his negligent behavior is deemed the cause of the accident. Thus, the individual will multiply the estimated potential damages done in an accident by the probability that his negligence will cause an accident when computing the costs and benefits of negligent behavior. The individual will compare the expected total cost of an accident due to his negligence with the expected benefits of negligent behavior, precisely as he should in order to efficiently utilize resources. If, at any point in time, an individual could avoid an accident but negligently does not, the law provides for that individual to be assessed the total damages, which, therefore, makes him responsible for the full marginal damage, which yields the proper marginal incentives at each step along the sequence of events leading to an accident. The final result will be that only one party will be found liable. The total liability is the total damages, giving the proper total incentives. In this way, the common law rule of negligence produces the proper incentives, both in total and at the margin.[16]

Two Recent Developments

There have been two recent legal developments that affect the rule of negligence as just described. The first is the no-fault rule, which has been legislated in some states, and the second is comparative negligence, which has been introduced by the coursts in some states. The no-fault rule, which applies only to automobile accidents, obviously implies inefficient incentives. The rule is a development of statutory law, and thus does not fall within the law-making framework discussed in this chapter. This rule is well criticized by Posner,[17] and need not be discussed here. The rest of this section will briefly discuss the doctrine of comparative negligence.

This doctrine divides the liability in negligence to correspond to the percentage of each party's negligence. Thus, if one party of an accident contributed 30 percent of the negligence to an accident, that party would be liable for 30 percent of the damages. This doctrine provides the proper total incentives,[18] since the total liability is equal to the total damages, but does not provide the proper marginal incentives. An individual who sees an accident developing, and also sees that another party is partially negligent, will have as an incentive to avoid the accident only a portion of the marginal damage that he might avoid, since he will be liable for only a portion of the damage of the accident. If the last clear chance doctrine were applicable and the individual could avoid the accident, he would have the proper incentive to exercise his chance. The theoretical analysis of this chapter would suggest that the precedent of the comparative negligence doctrine would be narrowed until it disappeared from the law.

Interestingly enough, the general opinion of lawyers has been that the rule of comparative negligence is preferable to the rule of contributory negligence.[19] This opinion is not based upon an analysis of efficient incentives implied within the law, but rather it is based on a concept of justice. As a general rule, it seems more just to share the assignment of liability for damages in negligence of each party involved in an accident. The concept of comparative negligence had a limited introduction via the courts in the 1850s.[20] Some court decisions in Georgia were based on the concept, and the doctrine of comparative negligence was subsequently enacted as a statute in that state. The concept was also introduced through the courts in Illinois at about the same time, but it was ultimately abandoned in the 1890s. Thus, the concept is a relatively old one, and has had ample occasion to establish itself as a part of the common law, yet has failed to do so. The failure of comparative negligence to be established as the law warrants closer attention due to the fact that the legal profession seems to prefer it as a general rule.

The failure of comparative negligence to become established as law is a good illustration of the point that an efficient law is more likely to be established when the law evolves on a case-by-case basis than when it is statutorily enacted as a general rule. Although the legal profession seems to believe that the comparative negligence doctrine is a better general rule, each specific case that arises seems to be better decided on the basis of the earlier-described negligence doctrine. This illustrates that the legal profession (of which judges are a part) is able to recognize and maintain an efficient set of rules when the law develops on a case-by-case basis, even though it does not recognize the general theory which makes the existing law operate to produce efficient decisions. If the legal profession had a choice of statutorily enacting the contributory negligence with last clear chance doctrine or the comparative negligence doctrine, it would almost surely choose the latter. A statutory choice in this case would probably select the law implying inefficient incentives, but the invisible hand of the common law has guided it toward the law with the efficient incentives.

In this light, some recent court decisions based on the comparative negligence doctrine raise some questions. If the comparative negligence rule is really inefficient, the theory in this chapter would predict that the precedent in those cases would be narrowed until they are no longer used. On the other hand, the recent cases in which the rule was used involved automobile accidents,[21] in which incentives may play a small (and uncertain) part, since the accidents happen so rapidly, and individuals might not reasonably be expected to exercise a "last clear chance," due to the likelihood of even a reasonable individual to panic or make an error in judgment when a split-second decision must be made. Thus, the new development of comparative negligence might be efficient in the case of automobile accidents, which is a circumstance that could not be foreseen when the negligence law was being developed. The law is currently in a state of change with respect to liability in automobile accidents, and so for this section to conclude with a statement about what the most efficient law would be would violate the spirit of the theoretical section of the chapter. While it would be relatively easy to examine a particular case to determine a law which implies proper incentives, to determine a general rule to apply to all cases is a task beyond the abilities of any one individual.

The purpose of this chapter is to explain some elements of efficiency in the way that the common law develops, and the development of the law as it relates to negligence has been used as an example. Some other writers have examined efficiency aspects of the rules of negligence and have concluded that the negligence doctrine is efficient.[22] But the emphasis here is on the process which is capable of producing efficient rules, rather than the efficient rules themselves, and the development of the negligence doctrine is intended to be illustrative of that process. Other writers have argued that the process is efficient also, although from slightly different standpoints.

Paul Rubin has developed a model in which parties have a continuing interest in the type of litigation that they bring to court.[23] Litigants in Rubin's model therefore have an interest in the case not only because of the outcome of the particular case (which could, after all, be settled out of court) but also in the precedent that will be applied to similar future cases, since the litigants would expect to be involved in similar future cases. Inefficient legal rules impose a higher social cost on society than efficient rules, making it more worthwhile to dispute inefficient rules in court. The result is that more inefficient rules will be considered than efficient rules, meaning that even if decisions are made randomly there will be a greater likelihood that inefficient rules will be overturned, and there will be a movement toward efficient laws. Rubin's conclusions are reinforced by a model of George Priest, who in a slightly different way concludes that inefficient rules are more likely to be challenged in court.[24] This line of reasoning is complementary to the analysis presented in this chapter. Rubin and Priest argue that inefficient rules are more likely to be challenged in court, while the argument in this chapter is that the common law process is better suited to finding the most efficient rule once the rule is challenged.

Conclusion

The legal profession has traditionally recognized the value of the adversary process in that it produces new law at the same time that it produces decisions in a particular case.[25] Despite their admiration for the process, students of the law have not developed a general theory explaining its efficiency. At the same time, many writers have seen efficient aspects of specific legal doctrines, or even the general efficiency of the entire body of the law,[26] but have focused on the efficiency of the existing legal doctrine rather than the efficiency of the process that produces that doctrine.[27] In a static sense, the law is a set of rules which governs the interactions of individuals within society; but in a dynamic sense the law is an institution which contains a mechanism for changing legal rules as the environment within which those rules operate changes.

An interesting feature of the common law is that although the existing doctrine was produced by a large number of court decisions, and is, therefore, the result of the action taken by a large number of judges, no single individual or group of individuals conceived of or planned the body of common law. Indeed, even a single rule in the common law is developed, modified, broadened, and qualified by many court decisions, so that the existing rule at any point in time is not the conscious design of any individual. Although nobody has planned the existing structure of the law, that structure was produced by the individual decisions of a large number of individuals. The common law is "a result of human action, but not of human design."[28]

Following the institutional approach used by Adam Smith, this chapter has viewed law as a process. The emphasis of the analysis has been on examining the efficiency of the institution rather than the efficiency of specific outcomes. Using this approach, the desirability of the outcomes of a process may be judged by the process, since efficient institutions will yield efficient results.

In this sense, the common law finds a close analog in the market sector of an economy. Available resources, productive techniques, and individual desires are very complex, and always changing. The market system provides an orderly institutional structure within which each individual can best use his own specialized knowledge; and by furthering his own best interest, he is led as if by an invisible hand to further the best interest of society. The common law provides an analogous situation with respect to the law. Individuals within the adversary process find it in their own self interest to develop and present the best legal arguments for their side of the case, and the system of precedent that is used to decide cases and define the law acts as an invisible hand which guides the law to follow the best interest of society.

The Democratic
Decision-making Process

This book has covered a great deal of diverse material, but all of it has been related to various aspects of the democratic decision-making process. At the foundation of democracy is the common law process and the implied social contract, so that although these chapters appeared last, their conclusions were implied in the earlier chapters that discussed the actual operation of the majority rule political system. Given this foundation, the earlier parts of the book that concentrated on decision making under majority rule focused more narrowly on the efficiencies and inefficiencies of majority rule decision making. An understanding of the capabilities of the political system can go a long way toward developing a consensus about the role of government in society. As suggested at the start of the book, most people are in general agreement concerning broad social goals. Almost everybody desires a prosperous economy where everybody can enjoy a comfortable standard of living, where the rights of individuals are protected, and most people favor friendly foreign relations. Almost everybody desires government policies that will promote an increasing standard of living and security in the future. The disagreement centers around the best policies to promote these common goals. The analysis of the capabilities of the political process may make some progress toward that end.

The primary purpose of this final chapter is to summarize the main points of the book and amplify the implications in order to develop the entire subject matter into a more coherent whole. The material has been diverse, but all has been related to the democratic decision-making process. The foundations were developed in the common law and social contract chapters, and upon this foundation is based the framework of the concepts of public sector equilibrium and Bowen's model of decision making under majority rule. It was within this framework that the efficiencies and inefficiencies of the political process were discussed. One purpose of this summary is to clarify the logical structure of these ideas.

The Foundations of Democracy

The bulk of the rules by which individuals interact in any society are not invented by specific individuals and are not passed into law at any particular time. They are rules that are the results of human action, but not of human design,[1] and gradually evolve as the society evolves. The theory of social Darwinism[2] hypothesizes that the efficient rules, and more broadly, the efficient institutions, will survive over time while inefficient rules and institutions will be weeded out. "The survival of the fittest" applies to social phenomena as well as biological phenomena.[3] This argument extends to the law, both as a rule-making institution and as a set of rules.

It is interesting to observe how the common law process has institutionalized the efficient evolution of legal rules in a manner analogous to the way that the market has institutionalized the efficient allocation of resources. An "invisible hand" guides the common law toward efficient outcomes. The foundation of common law must lie at the foundation of any democracy, simply because there are so many legal issues to be decided that no legislature could possibly pass a law to cover every situation that could arise. The sometimes very visible statute law passed by legislatures must be viewed as the tip of the figurative iceberg, resting on a less visible but far more significant foundation of common law.

Most of the issues discussed in this study have been regarding that tip of the iceberg, the legislative acts of a representative democracy and the resulting allocation of resources. A fundamental issue with respect to a representative democracy is how the power of those in the government can be justified. Some students of government assert that the monopoly over the use of force that governments possess cannot be justified, let alone all of the other types of monopolies (printing currency, delivering certain types of mail) that the government owns. One possible justification of the government's power is contained in the social contract theory of the state. Conceivably, everybody in a society could agree to yield some powers to a government, and the formation of such a government would constitute a Pareto superior move. Some readers might object that unanimous agreement does not constitute moral justification, but this normative argument will be put aside here in order to focus upon the difficulties with the social contract that occur farther down the logical chain.

In order for the social contract theory to be applicable to actual societies, the members of the society must have agreed with the terms of the contract. Since all of the members of the society did not actually agree to a social contract, and since in many societies the government is much older than its citizens (meaning that even if there was an original contract, the existing members were not party to it), some type of conceptual agreement must be fabricated if the theory is to have any connection with reality. Buchanan's concept of anarchistic equilibrium provides one method for hypothesizing agreement with the contract. Individuals compare the state of society with the possible states that they foresee could emerge if the contract were renegotiated from anarchy, and if the present society falls within the limits of what they might expect would emerge under a renegotiation of the contract, then those individuals would be in conceptual agreement with the existing social contract, as Buchanan defines conceptual agreement.

Using this construct, the social contract theory has some correspondence with the real world, and although there is no guarantee that a democratic government would be the result of the social contract, this is a method to justify the power of a democratic government as legitimate. Looking at the foundations of democracy in this way is enlightening because it reveals that even under the most favorable circumstances the government will be likely to alter the allocation of resources in its favor. The reason is that the power to change the rules under which society operates is a power of the government.

One might imagine a social contract being developed in a manner most favorable to the social contractarian, with a constitution written behind a veil of ignorance, in the sense that at the time the constitution is written, no person knows who will be an agent of the government and who will be a member of the private sector after the constitution is approved. Such a constitution would be likely to meet Buchanan's criterion for conceptual agreement with the contract, at least with respect to the relative privilege accruing to those inside and outside the government. The outcome would be likely to be in the middle of the expected range of renegotiation of the contract. But any contract that long endures must be flexible enough to change as circumstances change, and the mechanism for change will have to be through the government. The result is that each change in the contract is likely to favor those who enact the change, and the social contract will develop a bias in favor of the public sector.

Individuals within the private sector can do little to alleviate this bias, since any change in the contract must be enacted through government. An individual in the private sector who wants to be active in changing the terms of the contract must be elected or appointed to a position within the public sector, so the individual now has an incentive to be biased toward the public sector. Over time, the terms of the social contract will favor individuals in the public sector relative to those in the private sector. The writers of the American constitution were well aware of this tendency, which is why the constitution is primarily a document that limits the power of government.

Casual observation of contemporary societies reveals the tendencies suggested here. It is relatively easy to start new public sector programs and allocate additional resources through the public sector, and it is relatively difficult to halt the programs once they have begun. Any display of demand for additional governmental activity is rapidly met, but the government is not so responsive to decreases in demand for governmental activity. This includes both public sector programs and regulations that govern private sector activity. The reason why this is so, to emphasize, is that the people in the public sector are the people who make the rules.

A democratic constitution, written behind a veil of ignorance, seeks to minimize this bias through the use of majority rule. To use the American constitution as an example, the purpose of the constitution is to protect individual rights by limiting the power of the government. Majority rule is not intended to further the will of the majority, and so is not an end in itself. It is a means to the end of protecting individual rights by selecting the leaders of government, and it is a method by which those leaders can be periodically replaced in a peaceful and orderly manner. At the foundation of a democracy is a social contract that provides legitimacy to democratic institutions, and this foundation rests on the still broader base of the common law rules of society.

The reader who does not readily accept this social contract theory as the foundation of democracy should reflect for a moment on the actions of a democratic government and on the public's perception of those actions. There is the very popular myth that democratic governments are governments ultimately run by the voters, with elected representatives acting as their proxies. This myth is obviously false. Most voters are completely unaware of most of the business that the government undertakes, leaving their representatives free to be responsive to special interests and to other representatives with whom they might trade votes. Were a dictator to perform some of the acts that elected representatives in a democracy perform, there would undoubtedly be movements undertaken to replace him. Yet in a democracy these acts are accepted as legitimate. This is largely due to the implied social contract that recognizes the legitimacy of the representative's power because he was elected by a majority of the voters. The general public accepts this social contract, so that while there may be disagreement with the decisions a representative makes, the representative's exercise of power is rarely viewed as illegitimate.

If majority voting provides the legitimacy for the social contract in a democracy, then questions about the operation of a majority rule voting system are interesting both for their own sake and due to the more fundamental issues concerning the continuing social contract.

Resource Allocation under Majority Rule

Majority rule voting in a democracy might have a number of different ends as its ultimate goal. At one end of the spectrum, the actions that public sector officials may take could be closely specified by a constitution, including how choices must be made whenever such a situation arises. Majority rule could have as its object in this case only the selection of the official to perform the role specified in the constitution. If the role were specified closely enough, the presumption would be that anyone elected to the job would make the same choices and perform the same actions if the job were being done right. The role of majority rule in this extreme case would be to provide for an orderly succession of officeholders, and to provide for an easy method for replacing an officeholder who was not performing as expected.

At the other end of the spectrum, majority rule could be used to elect a dictator or a council of dictators to make decisions that would be binding on the citizens. Again, majority rule would provide for a method of replacing leaders who did not perform according to the expectations of voters. Somewhere between these two extremes, majority rule might also be used to allow voters to vote directly on collective decisions, making the government in effect a dictatorship of the majority. According to the median voter model as depicted by Bowen and Downs, these last two cases should provide identical policies, since the median voter's preference should be the outcome in either case. The first case should in theory be different, since a constitution could be written behind a veil of ignorance where, with respect to some issues anyway, individuals would not know on which side they would fall. Under these circumstances, majority coalitions would not be able to form in order to exploit minorities.

The point of this digression is to illustrate that majority rule can be used to select officials in a government that is guided by some fundamental principle other than majority rule. The United States Constitution, for example, was designed fundamentally to protect individual rights, and majority rule was seen as a means to that end rather than as an end in itself. Democratic election of governmental officials was seen as the best method for keeping the government from usurping the rights of individuals. A constrained majority rule can be much different from an unconstrained democracy.

Still, this distinction overemphasizes the differences among different types of democracies. No constitution can be foresighted enough to take account of every possible future development, so any constitution that will endure over time must be flexible enough to adapt to change. This gives the power to enact such changes to governmental officials, resulting in the bias described in the previous section. By the same token, our system of direct democracy will have to have provisions for only some individuals to have access to the agenda, again giving power to governmental officials. Elected officials must be responsive to the electorate in order to retain their jobs, but any system of democracy is automatically going to divide the citizenry into two groups: a small political elite, and a large group of citizens with no individual political power. Though as individuals they have no political power, the citizens have the collective power to select the political elite. The selection process may be biased toward incumbents since they make the election rules, and the greater the bias, the more the selection process becomes a mere symbol.

In practice, a democratic government is likely to be a combination of the types of democracies outlined at the beginning of this section. In some cases, governmental officials have the responsibility only to protect individual rights, guaranteed by the constitution. In other cases, they have the power to use their discretion in deciding what they think is the best decision to make without reference to popular opinion or to specific constitutional guidelines. In some instances, the voting public has the power to decide through referendum on specific issues. Generally, decisions by public officials will be guided partly by institutional factors, such as precedent or constitutional rules, partly by the opinions of the voters who have the power to unseat officials, and partly by the narrow self-interest of the decision maker. These motivating factors may be condensed even further. The institutional factors are important because voters perceive them to be so, and voter opinion is important because it is in the self-interest of the politician to receive the approval of the voters to remain in public office. In summary, then, public officials will make decisions that they believe will meet with the approval of the voters, except in instances when the benefits of making a different decision outweigh the value of the potential vote loss. The value of the potential vote loss will be small if the incumbent is almost certain to be reelected anyway, or if voters are uninformed or do not place much importance on the decision.

Seeing voters as the key to political decision making lies at the heart of the median voter model. The median voter model is a powerful simplifying device, because only the vote of the median voter is important. The median voter model is analytically powerful as a means for aggregating public sector demands, and it also does a good job of explaining political reality. Surely Richard Nixon's silent majority was the median voter.

In the simplest variant of the median voter model, all political decisions are made such that the median voter's most desired outcome results. This conception of democracy, developed by Hotelling, Bowen, and Downs, views the democratic decision-making process as a way in which the median voter dictates outcomes of political decisions. Much evidence supports this view of the democratic process, at least in particular instances. Some of this evidence is discussed in chapter 4. In addition, the election process can be designed to guarantee the outcome most preferred by the median voter, as described in chapter 5. The median voter model certainly is a valuable device for understanding public sector decision making, but even within the framework of the median voter model there are a number of reasons why the median voter's most preferred outcome may not result.

The Anatomy of Government Failure

Market failure is said to occur whenever resources are not allocated as they would be in a competitive equilibrium, and government failure might be similarly defined as the failure to allocate resources to produce a Bowen equilibrium. The analogy is not exact, since the Samuelson equilibrium is the Pareto optimal allocation, and the Bowen equilibrium allocation may differ from the Samuelson equilibrium. But the failure of a Bowen equilibrium to be a Samuelson equilibrium will not be discussed here, even though it could be an important consideration in the efficiency of the government's allocation of resources.

The factors causing government failure can be placed into two groups. The first group, most commonly discussed, is due to monopoly aspects of government. Less commonly discussed, but no less important are competitive aspects associated with political externalities. The monopoly problems with government will be reviewed first.

Most widely discussed in the economics literature are monopoly problems associated with government bureaucracies. Niskanen's perceptive analysis laid the groundwork by noticing the implications of the government budgetary process. Rather than purchasing incremental units of output from a bureaucracy, the bureaucracy's sponsor provides a total annual budget in exchange for a promise of a total output. Due to the superior bargaining position of the bureau, there is a tendency for bureaus to produce too much output. Niskanen and other analysts of government bureaucracies blame the incentive structure facing bureaucrats for this overproduction. The monopoly bureau is one of the key aspects of government bureaucracy that produces inefficient incentives, since no other agency may compete for an agency's budget by offering a different price or output mix. Indeed the formation of competing bureaus has been one frequently suggested possible improvement.

The economics literature to date has paid less attention to the problem of monopoly power held by elected officials. Part of this may be due to the competitive process for elective office described by the median voter model. While it is true that there is some competition between potential officeholders, majority rule politics in general has many of the characteristics of natural monopoly, because only one majority can exist at a time. Potential legislators find that there are large fixed costs involved in getting elected in order to produce legislation, but if successful, the average cost of producing additional legislation declines. Just as in other natural monopolies, legislators seek lump sum subsidies in order to satisfy their marginal conditions.

One of the implications of the natural monopoly situation is that new producers of legislation cannot enter the "industry" without driving an existing producer out of the industry. This provides a larger than usual incentive for producers of legislation to keep new entrants out of the industry. There is a natural reason, therefore, for a coalition to arise among incumbents and against challengers. Political competition has been traditionally pictured as arising between political parties, but over the longer term the most important part of political competition is the competition between incumbents and nonincumbents. Casual observation shows that states that are predominantly one-party states do not have less political competition than states with two parties of more equal strength. Instead, the weaker the second party, the more competitive the primary elections become. In general elections, especially at the national level, the competition between the incumbent from one party and the challenger from another party masks the fact that the true political competition is primarily between incumbent and challenger, and the fact that they are of different parties is only of secondary importance.

Consider an elected official in a minority party who has the opportunity to vote for measures that will enhance the chance of incumbents being reelected. The greater the chance that incumbents are reelected, the more likely it is that the politician's party will remain the minority party. After all, the only way that the politician's party can gain strength is by unseating incumbents from other parties. But making it more difficult for incumbents to be reelected will also increase the likelihood that this particular politician will be unseated. His choice is between increasing his party's chances of becoming the majority while decreasing his chances of reelection, or increasing his chances while making it more likely that his party will remain the minority party. All but the most secure candidates will opt for strengthening the power of incumbency, since belonging to the majority party will be of little benefit to the candidate if he is unseated. A majority party will be especially interested in increasing the ability of incumbents to be reelected, since it increases the likelihood of retaining the majority and benefits the individual party members at the same time. There is every incentive for a coalition of incumbents to form across party lines to oppose nonincumbents.

As incumbents enhance their collective ability to be reelected, some of the representativeness of the government is eroded. If, for instance, incumbents had a 100 percent probability of being reelected, the supposedly democratic government would in fact be a dictatorship by a committee of incumbents. Over time, the continuing social contract becomes something very different from a continually renegotiated social contract.

One consequence of the existence of politicians with monopoly power is that they have the ability to control the agendas of referenda presented to the electorate in order to affect their outcomes. Agenda control can be a very visible sign of the monopoly power of the agenda setter, but since so few issues in modern democracies are considered directly by the voters, it must be considered as a symptom of more deep-rooted problems. Monopoly power in government in general erodes the power of those not in government and diverts resources from the private to the public sector.

The perils of monopoly power in government are probably more obvious—and are certainly more widely discussed—than the adverse consequences of political competition. These adverse consequences arise because of an externality inherent in the majority rule voting process: a majority of the voters are able to make a decision which is binding on the minority. This means that any time a decision is made by less than unanimous approval, there will be some external cost paid by the majority. Competition for political office, however, biases these costs in favor of larger government expenditures.

This is the case because competitors for political office must compete for and win the vote of the median voter in order to be elected. A candidate could compete for the median vote by offering the median voter a lower tax share, which could be accomplished by raising the taxes of some other group of voters. With a lower tax share, the median voter's price per unit of government output will decline, and therefore the median voter's quantity demanded will increase. The Bowen equilibrium level of output will rise, causing larger government expenditures. Since this strategy is open to all candidates, competition for political office will force each candidate to offer to lower the median voter's tax share if the candidate wants the median voter's vote. The result is larger government expenditures.

The result is the same if the median voter is offered a larger share of public sector output without an increase in taxes. The price per unit of government output declines for the median voter, causing the median voter's quantity demanded to increase. By either lowering the median voter's tax share or increasing the median voter's benefit share, the quantity of public sector output demanded by the median voter will increase. The result is a larger Bowen equilibrium level of government expenditures. Because of the nature of majority rule voting, political competition can lead to an overexpansion of the public sector.

Possible Reforms

This work as a whole may appear to present a somewhat negative view of resource allocation through the public sector, but this was not the intention, and that appearance is as much the result of the methodology of the research as any other factor. In general, actual public sector outcomes have been compared to theoretical ideals rather than real-world alternatives, perhaps leading to an overly pessimistic tone in the same way that the market failure literature tends to present the market's ability to allocate resources in an unfavorable light. Certain governmental functions—police protection, courts, and national defense, for examples—appear to be natural candidates for governmental rather than private production.[4] The proper definition of government, perhaps, is the organization performing these functions. Other activities might be more effectively or cheaply designed and produced by government. Money production and a nationwide interstate highway system are two possible examples. But even these suggestions are open to debate, and in any event, the governmental structure must be considered as a candidate for reform, even among the strongest supporters of governmental activity. The potential changes discussed in this section are not necessarily the most urgent reforms, or even the most desirable. Considered in a broad extent, they may have drawbacks that would make some of them undesirable. They are discussed because they follow from the analysis presented earlier.

One of the main problems that occurs in a government over time is that those in power alter the nature of the social contract so that more power and more resources are allocated to the public sector. The government takes more resources than would be optimal from the private sector because the people who make the decisions concerning the amount of resources taken from the private sector and allocated to the public sector are public sector officials. Several corrective measures suggest themselves, though these measures have drawbacks of their own. One possibility is to have a limit to the number of terms that can be served by any officeholder. The president of the United States is limited to two terms, and that same limit might be appropriate for all other officeholders as well. The result would be that elected officials would not see themselves as a permanent part of the public sector, but as temporary officeholders who will return to the private sector. Although this reform would limit the experience of public officeholders, it would also be a way to guarantee that the legislature would not be able to evolve into an institution where incumbents continued to be reelected due to the power of the incumbency. Turnover of elected officials would be assured.

Another possible reform would be to limit the right to vote only to those citizens who contributed more to the government via direct tax payments than they received from the government through direct payments. This would include welfare recipients as well as government employees, as long as they received more than they contributed to the government. Under this reform, politicians would not be able to continually use direct transfers, government jobs, or raises to public employees as bribes for votes, since the recipients would not have the right to vote. Such a reform goes against the trend over the past several hundred years to extend the right to vote to a more inclusive group, and so assuredly is not politically feasible (or, perhaps, desirable) at this time. The ethical reasoning behind this reform, however, is that those who pay for the government have the right to determine how their money is spent and who is designated to spend it. But ethical reasons aside, this reform would undoubtedly result in a median voter with a smaller demand for government, simply because it reduces the possibilities of buying votes with government funds.

One of the problems noted in chapter 7 is that incumbents have an incentive to pass rules that keep nonincumbents from winning elections. The result is that incumbents are far more likely to win elections than challengers, strengthening the monopoly power of government officials. One way to combat this tendency would be to change the system of single-member districts—where incumbents never run against other incumbents—to a system of multimember districts, where several representatives are elected from each district. Each district might have, for example, four representatives. At election time, all four incumbents would run against each other as well as all challengers. The top four vote-getters would be elected. While this would lower the value of incumbency, it would also increase the heterogeneity of the group of representatives. Minor parties would find it easier to elect candidates, and the group of representatives would be less stable, both in terms of the individuals elected and the views held by representatives. The desirable and undesirable aspects are discussed at greater length in chapter 7.

Another reform that would limit the ability of political candidates to bribe voters for votes would be the adoption of a proportional tax structure. Any new programs would then have to be financed by all taxpayers in proportion to their existing tax burden, rather than more heavily by some groups than others. In addition, no politician could propose to lower the median voter's tax burden by raising the taxes of other voters. Such a strategy was the subject of chapter 6. The drawback to implementation of this reform is the redistributional implications, although these issues may not be as great as they would first seem, since lower tax rates to high income earners would give those individuals with the highest marginal products additional incentives to produce.

One way to make the government more responsive to the demands of its constituents would be to hold more referenda to let voters directly decide how they would like public sector resources allocated. Some issues may not be well suited to referenda, and issues that would abridge constitutional rights would certainly be unsuitable. The most obvious candidates for referenda would be the size and distribution of the government budget. Chapter 5 explained the Florida system, which would be a good method for holding referenda on public sector expenditures. By holding referenda in this way, the size and distribution of the government budget would be determined directly by the voters, leaving the details to the officials who presently make those decisions. The government budget would be more responsive to voters, and have less room for allocation to special interests and programs aimed specifically at winning the vote of the median voter. Holding more referenda would be technically feasible, and is a method for making the government more responsive to the demands of its citizens.

Probably the soundest reform that could be enacted would be the requirement that every expenditure program voted by the legislature would have to include in it a tax program that would state where the funds will come from to finance the expenditures. This way, the costs of programs would be clearly stated and approved along with the expenditures, and the legislature would be forced to consider the costs and benefits of programs simultaneously. When spending programs can be approved without simultaneously determining where the revenues will come from, there is a tendency for politicians to enact popular programs that will provide benefits to their constituencies without simultaneously enacting unpopular taxation programs. Since every program to spend money logically implies that the same amount of revenues be raised, the requirement that taxing and spending programs be determined simultaneously is simply a requirement that the legislature simultaneously consider the costs and benefits of its actions. Legislators would probably be against such a proposal, but aside from this (powerful) opposition, the proposal would seem to benefit everyone by forcing the legislature to be more responsible in making spending decisions. This reform would seem to have few drawbacks, and would go a long way toward promoting fiscal responsibility by the government.

The reforms listed here are by no means exhaustive, and may not even be the most worthwhile reforms. Some, in fact, may be undesirable when all of their costs and benefits are considered. Those reforms are listed because they are suggested by the analysis in earlier chapters. The problems described earlier are real problems, so perhaps these reforms could be developed and modified to be suitable solutions to some of the problems facing democratic governments. Governments provide valuable services, but nobody can deny that there is ample room for improvement in the way in which the government allocates resources.

Conclusion

There are several reasons why a work such as this might be valuable. One might optimistically hope that a better understanding of the way in which the public sector operates could promote reforms that would improve resource allocation. But a simple understanding itself could be beneficial because it could promote a more general agreement on the role that the government can play in pursuing various social goals. The point was made before—but it is worth emphasizing—that most people share the same general social goals of a comfortable standard of living for all, for helping the less fortunate members of society, for promoting progress so that the society will be even better off in the future. Most disagreement is not over what general social goals are desirable, but rather over what are the best methods for achieving those goals. With respect to government policy, the extreme views are on the one hand that all resources should be allocated through the market, since the market most efficiently allocates resources and also is the most effective provider of opportunity to the less privileged members of society; and on the other hand that the allocation of resources should be primarily controlled by the government to provide an equitable distribution of income and so that resources can be allocated according to a central plan that takes account of the social welfare rather than private interests.

The disagreement here is essentially positive rather than normative, since the general social goals are widely agreed upon, and the disagreement is over the most effective way to achieve the goals.[5] The topics covered in this book are especially relevant to this debate because the book has been primarily concerned with the capabilities of government, and in particular with the capability of a democratic decision-making process to efficiently allocate resources. The government is certainly capable of pursuing many social goals, and such goods and services as the production of law and order, the orderly settlement of disputes through the court system, the network of public roads, and public education system demonstrate the capability of government in a number of diverse areas. The government has not fared so well in other areas, such as the war on poverty, or the production of stable prices and low unemployment.

Though some social goals might be held as desirable by almost everyone, the society must at the same time recognize the possibility that the government may not be capable of achieving these goals. The preceding chapters have examined some aspects of the capabilities of majority rule governments and found some definite limitations. In government policy, as in anything else, good intentions are not enough. Social goals cannot be achieved simply because they are held as generally desirable. The social system must also have the capability to achieve those goals. The best method will not generally be to provide a government agency with a lot of money with the hope that it will be able to buy a solution to the problem.

The problems with resource allocation through the public sector that have been noted throughout the book have been mostly due to the incentive structure that exists within the public sector. Government agencies in general have the incentive to maximize budgets rather than the profits that are maximized in the market. Instead of the efficiency paralleling the market, the result is government budgets that are too large. The other major aspect of the public sector incentive structure is the incentive of candidates for elective office to win a majority of the votes in order to be elected. Much of this book has been devoted to analyzing some problems that arise when resources are allocated by majority rule.

The framework of this analysis has been from within the median voter model, and although that model was greatly modified in the analysis, it always retained the basic feature that in a majority rule system it is necessary to capture the vote of the median voter in order to win the election. The logic of the median voter model seems to be reflected in political reality. Not only does the model have predictive value, but candidates themselves seem to recognize that some voters will clearly vote for them, some will clearly not, and that they must campaign to the median group whose votes determine the election outcome. The assumption of a single-dimensioned continuum of political preferences seems to reflect contemporary political reality.

One characteristic of this political reality is that under a majority rule system of government, it is the voter who cares the least that determines the outcome of an election. Voters with strong preferences, who are toward the ends of the continuum, do not cast the crucial votes. The votes that determine the outcome of an electron are votes toward the median, and these votes are cast by the voters with the least intense preferences. This fact, explored in some detail in chapter 6, might promote additional exploration with which to close this book.

The median voter, who casts the decisive vote, is the "policeman" of the political marketplace in the sense that it is the median voter who weighs the advantages of each candidate in order to determine who would be most suitable for office. Compare the median voter with the marginal consumer who polices the economic marketplace. Although the assumption that all participants are fully informed is frequently made for convenience in market models, it is unnecessary, since only the marginal consumers need be informed in order to police the market. How big that margin need be is not directly relevant here; the point is that many customers can purchase products without reference to brand name or firm reputation because the marginal customers make informed choices, so that firms producing inferior products (considering the price) lose customers and can no longer compete with the more efficient producers. Efficient firms survive and inefficient firms do not because informed consumers will choose to purchase from efficient producers. These consumers are the marginal consumers who will search for the best terms the market has to offer.

The marginal consumer in the market will tend to be one who purchases regularly in the market, and who makes relatively large purchases, since it is worthwhile for this type of consumer to seek information. The consumer who cares the most will be the policeman of the market, then, while consumers who have relatively small demands are more likely to buy with relatively little information, assuming (with justification) that competition will have weeded out the relatively inefficient producers. In the market, then, the consumers who care the most act as policemen to keep an efficient allocation of resources.

Many other informational problems with the political market have been discussed, from the fact that voters will be rationally ignorant concerning political choices because the voter's single vote will not alter the outcome of an election to the incentives that special interests have to influence legislation while nobody has a counterbalancing incentive to represent the general public interest. The problem with the policing mechanism in the political marketplace is related, because voters do not have an incentive to gather information. (Individuals will be informed about politics for the same reason they are informed about sports—because they are privately interested—not because their opinions will make them more effective political consumers.) The informational problem with the policing mechanism, though, is that the voter who is least interested in the outcome of an election is the one who determines the outcome. In the market, by contrast, the most interested consumers are the policemen.

In evaluating the capabilities for the public sector to efficiently allocate resources, an important aspect is the policing mechanism. Who performs the role of evaluating the performances of elected officials? In a democracy, it is the voter who cares the least who casts the decisive vote.[6] In view of the low incentives for gathering political information, it certainly appears that public sector resource allocation is policed less effectively than private sector resource allocation.

While some reforms may be in order, simple recognition of the strengths and weaknesses of allocating resources through the public sector may ultimately be the greatest contributor to public sector efficiency. With this knowledge, public sector resources can be invested in those areas where the incentive structure suggests an advantage in public over private production. At the same time, the government will have the opportunity to stop allocating resources to those areas where the incentive structure promotes inefficiency. Since politicians are ultimately responsible to the ballot box, information needs to be disseminated to voters as well as politicians if it is to have any impact on the political process. This task is compounded by the difficulty that, unlike in the marketplace, the least interested voters play an important role. The hope lies with future political entrepreneurs. To initiate beneficial changes, they will have to possess the insight that an economically efficient change leaves more surplus to be distributed among potential voters, as well as the ability to persuade voters of the validity of their case.

NOTES
BIBLIOGRAPHY
INDEX

NOTES

Chapter 1. Introduction

1. See James M. Buchanan's "Public Finance and Public Choice," *National Tax Journal* 28 (Dec. 1975): 383–94, for an elaboration of this theme.

2. John Maynard Keynes, *The General Theory of Employment, Interest and Money* (New York: Harcourt, Brace, 1936).

3. For another perspective of Keynes's influence, see James M. Buchanan and Richard E. Wagner, *Democracy in Deficit: The Political Legacy of Lord Keynes* (New York: Academic Press, 1977).

4. A.C. Pigou, *The Economics of Welfare,* 4th ed. (London: Macmillan, 1932). Adam Smith, *The Wealth of Nations* (New York: Random House, Modern Library, 1937), discusses the way in which taxes should be assigned to finance the assistance that government provides to private enterprise. Smith notes, "The expense of government to the individuals of a great nation, is like the expense of management to the joint tennants of a great estate, who are all obligated to contribute in proportion to their respective interests in the estate" (p. 777).

5. See, for example, Francis M. Bator, "The Anatomy of Market Failure, *Quarterly Journal of Economics* 72 (Aug. 1958): 351–79; and Paul A. Samuelson, "The Pure Theory of Public Expenditure" *Review of Economics and Statistics* 36 (Nov. 1954): 387–89.

6. This theme is developed by Buchanan, "Public Finance and Public Choice."

7. Keynes, *The General Theory,* p. 383.

8. This point was made by Friedrich A. Hayek, *The Road to Serfdom* (London: George Routledge & Sons, 1944), and by David Friedman, "Many, Few, One: Social Harmony and the Shrunken Choice Set," *American Economic Review* 70, no. 1 (Mar. 1980): 225–32.

9. See James M. Buchanan, "An Economic Theory of Clubs," *Economica* (Feb. 1965), pp. 1–14.

10. Ayn Rand, *The Virtue of Selfishness* (New York: New American Library, 1961). Chapter 14 argues that police protection, national defense, and courts are the only legitimate functions of government.

11. Without government, anarchy might be a Hobbesian jungle, but Murray Rothbard, in *For a New Liberty* (New York: Macmillan, 1973),

argues that anarchy would be orderly and productive because private enterprise would efficiently produce those services now produced by government.

Chapter 2. Concepts of Public Sector Equilibrium

1. For an elaboration of this point, See Buchanan, "Public Finance and Public Choice."

2. Paul A. Samuelson, "The Pure Theory of Public Expenditure," *Review of Economics and Statistics* 36 (Nov. 1954): 387–89; and idem, "A Diagrammatic Exposition of a Theory of Public Expenditure," *Review of Economics and Statistics* 37 (Nov. 1955): 350–56.

3. Erik Lindahl, "Just Taxation—A Positive Solution" (1919), in Richard A. Musgrave and Alan T. Peacock, eds., *Classics in the Theory of Public Finance* (New York: St. Martin's Press, 1967), pp. 168–76.

4. Samuelson, "The Pure Theory" and "A Diagramatic Exposition."

5. The satisfaction of this condition has been called a Samuelson equilibrium before the writing of this book, however. See, for example, T. Nicolaus Tideman and Gordon Tullock, "A New and Superior Process for Making Social Choices," *Journal of Political Economy* 84 (Dec. 1976): 1156.

6. Samuelson, "The Pure Theory," pp. 388–89. These difficulties, at least in theory, are not insurmountable. See Tideman and Tullock, "A New and Superior Process," and the articles cites therein for possible solutions.

7. This point has been made by James M. Buchanan, in *The Demand and Supply of Public Goods* (Chicago: Rand McNally, 1968), chap. 4, and in his "Notes for an Economic Theory of Socialism," *Public Choice* 8 (Spring 1970): 29–43. The point was also made by Robin Barlow, in "Efficiency Aspects of Local School Finance: Reply," *Journal of Political Economy* 81 (Jan.–Feb. 1973): 199–202.

8. Harold Hotelling, "Stability in Competition," *Economic Journal* 39 (Mar. 1929): 41–57; and Howard R. Bowen, "The Interpretation of Voting in the Allocation of Economic Resources," *Quarterly Journal of Economics* 58 (Nov. 1943): 27–48.

9. This variant of the model is explained by Bowen and is considered in far more detail in Duncan Black, *The Theory of Committees and Elections* (Cambridge: Cambridge University Press, 1958).

10. Kenneth J. Arrow, *Social Choice and Individual Values*, 2nd ed. (New Haven and London: Yale Univ. Press, 1963).

11. The empirical evidence on the median voter model is reviewed in chapter 4.

12. In the specific example graphed in Figure 2.1, the median voter's tax price equals MC/5.

13. This derivation appears in the author's "The Florida System: A Bowen Equilibrium Referendum Process," *National Tax Journal* 30 (Mar. 1977): 77–84.

14. See, however, Tideman and Tullock, "A New and Superior Process for Making Social Choices," for a description of a possible institutional framework for producing Samuelson equilibrium.

15. For an English translation, see Lindahl, "Just Taxation—A Positive Solution."

16. Richard A. Musgrave, *The Theory of Public Finance* (New York: McGraw-Hill, 1959) p. 76, calls the T_is "unit prices."

17. Arthur T. Denzau and Robert J. Mackay, "Benefit Shares and Majority Voting," *American Economic Review* 66 (Mar. 1976): 69–76.

18. Knut Wicksell, "A New Principle of Just Taxation" (1896), in Musgrave and Peacock, eds., *Classics in the Theory of Public Finance,* pp. 72–118.

19. As a practical matter, Wicksell recommended an approximate unanimity of less than 100 percent approval, while recognizing the desirability in principle of the unanimous rule. James M. Buchanan and Gordon Tullock, in *The Calculus of Consent* (Ann Arbor: Univ. of Michigan Press, 1962), chap. 6, suggest that a less than unanimous decision rule could win the unanimous approval of a group.

20. The characteristics of Wicksellian unanimity have been extensively analyzed by James M. Buchanan. See, for examples, his "Politics, Policy, and the Pigouvian Margins," *Economica* n.s. 29 (Feb. 1962): 17–28; and "The Relevance of Pareto Optimality," *Journal of Conflict Resolution* (Nov. 1962), pp. 341–54. The latter also appears as chap. 15 in Buchanan's *Freedom in Constitutional Contract* (College Station: Texas A&M Univ. Press, 1977).

21. Charles M. Tiebout, "A Pure Theory of Local Expenditures," *Journal of Political Economy* 64 (Oct. 1956): 416–24.

22. This adjustment mechanism has sometimes been described as "voting with your feet." For a discussion of the limitations of the Tiebout process, see James M. Buchanan and Charles J. Goetz, "Efficiency Limits of Fiscal Mobility: An Assessment of the Tiebout Model," *Journal of Public Economics* 1 (1972): 25–43.

23. Tideman and Tullock, as already noted, have recently described another mechanism for producing Samuelson equilibrium but without requiring mobility of individuals. The system is a complex voting process that has nice theoretical properties but could be complicated to implement. The fact that this type of article appeared over twenty years after Samuelson's article suggests the magnitude of the theoretical problem of demand revelation that Samuelson noted.

24. A similar theme is developed in Buchanan's "Notes for an Economic Theory of Socialism."

25. Milton Friedman's "The Role of Government in Education," in *Capitalism and Freedom* (Chicago: Univ. of Chicago Press, 1962), is the classic argument for a voucher system.

26. The concept was originally presented in William A. Niskanen's "The Peculiar Economics of Bureaucracy," *American Economic Review* 58 (May 1968): 293–305; and additional implications appear in his *Bureaucracy and Representative Government* (Chicago and New York: Aldine-Atherton, 1971). Niskanen subsequently made some modifications to his original model in "Bureaucrats and Politicians," *Journal of Law and Economics* 18 (Dec. 1975): 617–43.

27. For conflicting views on the value of Niskanen's contribution, see Earl A. Thompson, "Review of Niskanen's *Bureaucracy and Representative Government,*" *Journal of Economic Literature* 11 (Sept. 1973): 950–53; and Gordon Tullock, "Review of Niskanen's *Bureaucracy and Representative Government,*" *Public Choice* 12 (Spring 1972): 119–24.

28. Anthony Downs, in "Why the Government Budget is too Small in a Democracy," *World Politics* 12 (July 1960): 541–64, argues that the opposite is true.

29. The problem of incentives for public sector officials was clearly recognized by Bowen and Tiebout, but their models still amount to a demand aggregation process. This is why Buchanan and Goetz questioned the existence of incentives in the Tiebout model.

30. Models of agenda control in public sector referenda have yielded results similar to Niskanen's, but these models are models of demand manipulation. They are not discussed here since the next chapter will be devoted to them.

31. Lindahl did develop the concept within a hypothetical institutional framework, but as used in the current literature, Lindahl equilibrium is devoid of institutional content.

Chapter 3. Agenda Control in the Median Voter Model

1. See Thomas Romer and Howard Rosenthal, "Political Resource Allocation, Controlled Agendas, and the Status Quo," *Public Choice* 33, no. 4 (1978): 27–43.

2. See Duncan Black, *The Theory of Committees and Elections* (Cambridge: Cambridge Univ. Press, 1958), for a discussion of the problems that arise from relaxing this assumption.

3. See J.R. Hicks, *Value and Capital,* 2nd edition (Oxford: Oxford Univ. Press, 1946), p. 92.

4. The voter's preferences are illustrated with both the utility function and the marginal valuation curve because both will be used in the course of the analysis. Although the utility function is more elegant (and

perhaps more rigorous) than the marginal valuation curve, the use of the marginal valuation curve will frequently simplify the analysis.

5. Process efficiency means that the output produced could not have been produced at a smaller resource cost. This term was coined by Niskanen in *Bureaucracy and Representative Government.*

6. These sources of efficiency are excluded in order to ensure that the issue is not decided before the election. This would be realistic when the number of voters is large.

7. Chapter 6 discusses the implications of allowing politicians to determine the proportion of total taxes to be paid by each taxpayer.

8. Anthony Downs, in *An Economic Theory of Democracy* (New York: Harper & Row, 1957), explains this material in more detail.

9. Niskanen, *Bureaucracy and Representative Government*, chap. 5.

10. The model was developed in the form in which it appears in this chapter in Randall G. Holcombe, "A Public Choice Analysis of Millage Issue Elections for Financing Public Schools" (Ph.D. diss., Virginia Polytechnic Institute and State University, 1975). It was independently developed in an unpublished paper by Thomas Romer and Howard Rosenthal. Subsequent published works include Romer and Rosenthal's previously cited "Political Resource Allocation, Controlled Agendas, and the Status Quo," and "Bureaucrats Versus Voters: On the Political Economy of Resource Allocation by Direct Democracy," *Quarterly Journal of Economics* 93, no. 4 (Nov. 1979): 563–87; and Randall G. Holcombe, "An Empirical Test of the Median Voter Model," *Economic Inquiry* 18, no. 2 (Apr. 1980): 260–74.

11. A number of examples are listed in Robert J. Mackay and Carolyn L. Weaver, "Monopoly Bureaus and Fiscal Outcomes: Deductive Models and Implications for Reform," in Gordon Tullock and Richard E. Wagner, eds., *Policy Analysis and Deductive Reasoning* (Lexington, Mass.: D.C. Heath, Lexington Books, 1978), pp. 141–65.

12. James M. Buchanan and Marilyn Flowers, "An Analytic Setting for a Taxpayers' Revolution," *Western Economic Journal* 7 (Dec. 1969): 349–59. See also Raymond Jackson, "A 'Taxpayers' Revolution' and Economic Rationality," *Public Choice* 10 (Spring 1971): 93–96.

13. James M. Buchanan, "The Economics of Earmarked Taxes," *Journal of Political Economy* 71 (Oct. 1963): 457–69; and idem, *Public Finance and Democratic Process* (Chapter Hill: Univ. of North Carolina Press, 1967).

14. Charles R. Plott and Michael E. Levine, "A Model of Agenda Influence on Committee Decision," *American Economic Review* 68, no. 1 (Mar. 1978): 146–60.

15. In the type of agenda control that manipulates the order, the voters' generally preferred option is eliminated from the final vote through agenda control.

16. Mackay and Weaver, in "Monopoly Bureaus and Fiscal Outcomes," discuss the control of benefit shares. See also Denzau and Mackay, "Benefit Shares and Majority Voting."

17. The skeptical reader may turn ahead to chapter 6 for the complete argument.

18. Benefit shares could not be altered in the case of a pure Samuelsonian good, of course, but the control of tax shares would be a possibility in any case.

Chapter 4. An Empirical Test of the Median Voter Model

1. These sections are based upon Randall G. Holcombe, "An Empirical Test of the Median Voter Model," *Economic Inquiry* 18, no. 2 (Apr. 1980): 260–74.

2. This amount varies from district to district.

3. Data used in this section are taken from *Operational Millage Issue and Bond Issue Report* (SM-4375) of June 1973, the same *Report* for June 1972, and from *Ranking of Michigan High School Districts by Selected Financial data*, 1972–73, all published by the Michigan Department of Education.

4. In Michigan, millage rates for financing public schools are subdivided into three distinct categories: operation, building and site, and debt retirement. This section refers only to operational millage rates, which bypasses the interest rate and time discount problems involved in the other two categories.

5. The data used in this section is taken from *Operational Millage Issue and Bond Issue Report* (SM-4375) of June 1973, and from *Ranking of Michigan High School Districts by Selected Financial Data*, 1972–73. The 257 elections used as data for this section represent all elections for which data are included in both of the above publications. Thus, elections were omitted from this analysis only due to unavailable data.

6. See, for example, Robin Barlow, "Efficiency Aspects of Local School Finance," *Journal of Political Economy* 78 (Sept.–Oct. 1970): 1028–40; Theodore C. Bergstrom and Robert Goodman, "Private Demand for Public Goods," *American Economic Review* 63 (June 1973): 280–96; and Thomas E. Borcherding and Robert T. Deacon, "The Demand for Services of Non-Federal Governments," *American Economic Review* 62 (Dec. 1972): 891–901.

7. The school board would have an incentive to try to conceal possible alternatives that might be offered in the event of a failure, in order to reinforce the appearance of a two-point offer and thus increase the probability that the present referendum will pass.

8. The assumed distribution of preferences may be chosen indepen-

dently of the assumed shape of the demand curves since the distribution of preferences includes only one point (the voter's most preferred point) from each voter's demand function. The concept of the distribution of preferences is used in the same manner in this chapter as it was used by Downs *(An Economic Theory of Democracy)* in his exposition of the median voter model. A normal distribution is assumed because, as will be evident later, the data allow only two points on the distribution of preferences to be known. Thus, in order to specify completely the distribution of preferences, a two-parameter distribution must be used. In the absence of more information, the normal distribution seems to be the most reasonable two-parameter distribution to use.

9. In all four cases, the election results were close to each other. The results may not have conformed to the predictions of the model for a number of reasons. Preferences may have changed between elections; or, more likely, some other factor affected the composition of voter turnout. Different timing of elections, different interest group support or election campaigns, as well as other unrelated issues appearing on the same ballot, may have affected turnout. Similar factors might affect all elections under study, but there is no reason to suspect that they bias the results in one direction. When looking at the data as a whole, therefore, these effects may be assumed to offset each other.

10. Representative examples would include Theodore C. Bergstrom and Robert Goodman, "Private Demand for Public Goods," and Thomas E. Borcherding and Robert T. Deacon, "The Demand for Services of Non-Federal Governments."

11. James L. Barr and Otto A. Davis, "An Elementary Political and Economic Theory of the Expenditures of Local Governments," *Southern Economic Journal* 33 (Oct. 1966): 149–65.

12. Robert P. Inman, "Testing Political Economy's 'as if' Assumption: Is the Median Income Voter Really Decisive?" *Public Choice* 33, no. 4 (1978): 45–65.

13. William A. McEachern, "Collective Decision Rules and Local Debt Choice: A Test of the Median Voter Hypothesis," *National Tax Journal* 31, no. 2 (June 1978): 129–36.

14. Thomas Romer and Howard Rosenthal, "Bureaucrats Versus Voters: On the Political Economy of Resource Allocation by Direct Democracy."

Chapter 5. The Florida System: A Bowen Equilibrium Referendum Process

1. This chapter is largely based upon Randall G. Holcombe, "The Florida System: A Bowen Equilibrium Referendum Process," *National Tax Journal* 30 (Mar. 1977): 74–84.

2. In addition to operational expenditures, schools also raise revenues for debt retirement, capital improvements, and a number of other categories in many states. Categories, as well as the method of raising revenue, vary from state to state.

3. See Holcombe, "A Public Choice Analysis of Millage Issue Elections for Financing Public Schools," chap. 4 for a more detailed discussion of the different referendum procedures among the states.

4. In some states a rate that is passed remains until it is repeated in a referendum. In other states, millage rates can only be approved for a certain number of years, and then must be renewed. Thus, in some cases, the addition to the millage rate may be only a renewal of the expired former rate.

5. In this sample ballot, ten mills was chosen as the school board's proposed rate. Usually, a referendum for capital improvements would appear on the same ballot. The form of the ballot varies slightly depending upon whether paper ballots or voting machines are used, but voters are offered the same choices in either case. The referendum law is contained in Title 15-236.32 of the Florida state code.

6. An exception to this statement is the case where the voter's preferences are double peaked, the median lies between the two peaks, and the bottom of the trough lies between the voter's global maximum and the median voter's maximum. In this case, the voter would be better off selecting his local maximum rather than his global maximum preference. This solution would probably suggest itself to the voter, and so should not affect the analysis. However, there are collective choice methods that do not require single-peaked preferences. For the description of one such system, see T. Nicolaus Tideman and Gordon Tullock, "A New and Superior Process for Making Social Choices."

7. See, for example, Edward H. Clarke, "Multipart Pricing of Public Goods," *Public Choice* 2 (Fall 1971): 17–33, and the discussion of Clarke's system of Tideman and Tullock, "A New and Superior Process for Making Social Choices."

8. Under majority rule, an individual vote would be almost worthless, and thus could be bought at a relatively low price, since it would not by itself change the outcome of the election. Stated differently, the marginal value of a vote would be less than its average value if enough votes were purchased to change the outcome of the election. Individuals who take the behavior of other potential vote sellers as given, even if they had perfect information, would be willing to sell their votes at less than their average value. Therefore, individuals who are in the majority could rationally sell their votes, lose the election, and be worse off, due to the

prisoner's dilemma game-like nature of vote selling under majority rule. This would not be as likely under the Florida system, where each vote affects the outcome of the election, so that the average value of each vote equals the marginal value. Therefore, it would be far more expensive to "purchase" the outcome of an election in the Florida system than under majority rule.

9. I am indebted to Gilbert Gentry, chief of the Bureau of Finance and Management Services, Florida Public Schools, for supplying statistical and institutional information on public education financing in Florida.

10. Data on the number of mills appearing on the district ballot (recommended by the school board) was not available at the state level. The state records only the results of the referenda. Thus, information about district elections had to be collected from the individual district.

11. In Michigan, for instance, about 65 percent of the referenda pass; and in California only about 50 percent are approved. This could be due to the fact that the Florida system picks the exact Bowen equilibrium rate, so that last year's exact median preference is known. In other referendum states, the Bowen rate is only approximately selected; thus, Florida school boards have better information on the preferences of their voters.

12. See Knut Wicksell, "A New Principle of Just Taxation," in Richard A. Musgrave and Alan T. Peacock, eds., *Classics in the Theory of Public Finance* (New York: St. Martin's Press, 1967), pp. 72–118.

13. Buchanan and Flowers, in "An Analytic Setting for a Taxpayers' Revolution," addressed this issue some time ago, suggesting the basis for taxpayer dissatisfaction.

14. These were the words used by Milton Friedman in his television series "Free to Choose." Milton Friedman and Rose Friedman, in *Free to Choose* (New York: Harcourt Brace Jovanovich, 1980), p. 265, convey the same idea.

15. The next two sections are based upon "Tax Referenda and the Voluntary Exchange Model of Taxation: A Suggested Implementation," by Randall G. Holcombe and Paul C. Taylor, from *Public Finance Quarterly* 8 (Jan. 1980): 107–14, used with permission of the publisher, Sage Publications, Beverly Hills.

16. See Martin Bronfenbrenner, "A Percentage Budget for Public Appropriations," *National Tax Journal* 18 (Dec. 1965), 375–79; and Holcombe, "The Florida System," for earlier references to this type of voting.

17. See, for examples, Theodore Groves, "Incentives in Teams," *Econometrica* 41 (July 1973): 617–33; Tideman and Tullock, "A New and Superior Process for Making Social Choices"; Clarke, "Multipart Pricing

of Public Goods"; and Earl A. Thompson, "A Pareto-Optional Group Decision Process," *Papers on Nonmarket Decision Making* 1 (1965): 133–40. For an overview of some of the issues, see T. Nicolaus Tideman, "The Capabilities of Voting Rules in the Absence of Coalitions," in T.N. Clarke, ed., *Citizen Preferences and Urban Public Policy* (Beverly Hills: Sage Publications, 1976), pp. 23–44.

18. Tideman, in "The Capabilities of Voting Rules," notes that some incentive problems may arise when categories of goods are viewed as complements or substitutes to each other in a multidimensional setting.

19. If refunds were determined by all other voters' ballots but the ones getting the refund, there would be an incentive to vote for no refund, which would tax others the maximum amount.

Chapter 6. Public Choice and Public Spending

1. The remainder of this chapter is based upon Randall G. Holcombe, "Public Choice and Public Spending," *National Tax Journal* 31 (Dec. 1978): 373–83.

2. This assumption is introduced in order to lend stability to the final equilibrium, because in the absence of restrictions on the type of platform that can be offered by parties, there always exists a platform that two out of three groups will prefer to any existing platform. See Buchanan and Tullock, *The Calculus of Consent*, chap. 11, for a discussion of stability in simple game-theoretic voting models.

3. This assumption is included in order to preclude the solution where one party proposes to have opposing party members shoulder the entire tax burden. Without this assumption, the basic conclusion of the model would still hold, but the solution would not be realistic. Later discussion will explain why parties may find it in their best interest to tax their own members a rate above the average tax rate.

4. This analysis ignores income effects and thus treats demand curves as equivalent to marginal valuation curves. In addition, the average cost of government is assumed to be constant for any level of output.

5. Examples of constitutionally given tax shares are the proportional property taxes and sales taxes. The possibility of having the property tax structure be progressive with respect to the value of a home certainly exists but is considered constitutionally given and is not a campaign issue. Fixed income tax shares would also be possible but are not at this time constitutionally given.

6. His most preferred level of output could rise, and at the same time his most preferred budget size could fall, depending upon his elasticity of demand for government output. For a discussion of the effects of demand elasticities on the most preferred level of government expen-

ditures, see Denzau and Mackay, "Benefit Shares and Majority Voting," and Buchanan, "The Economics of Earmarked Taxes."

7. A formal statement of the idea sketched in this example appears in Denzau and Mackay, "Benefit Shares and Majority Voting," and therefore will not be reproduced here.

8. Many of these ideas are sketched by George J. Stigler, in "Director's Law of Public Income Redistribution," *Journal of Law and Economics* 13 (Apr. 1970): pp. 1–10, who notes, "The increase in the flexibility of taxes and expenditure programs works toward a larger role for government, and toward programs which redistribute income increasingly toward lower income classes."

9. This assumes that there are only two parties. Downs, in *An Economic Theory of Democracy,* pp. 123–24, explains why the equilibrium number of parties in the American political system is two. If the Libertarian party arose as a third party in this model, it would have to share votes received by the low demand party but would not reduce the votes received by the high demand party. This would reduce even more the likelihood of a victory by the low demand party, and the parties would eventually merge, or one would collapse.

Chapter 7. Elements of Monopoly in Government

1. In his classic article, Francis M. Bator ("The Anatomy of Market Failure") notes the monopoly problem as a possible shortcoming of the market. Friedman and Friedman, in *Free to Choose,* suggest that most monopolies are caused by government intervention, however.

2. Jonathan R.T. Hughes, in *The Governmental Habit* (New York: Basic Books, 1977), suggests that the government has always been used to limit competition in the private sector. See also Friedman and Friedman *(Free to Choose),* who concur with Hughes.

3. Centralization of governmental activity has been criticized by Niskanen, in *Bureaucracy and Representative Government,* on these grounds.

4. This section of this chapter is based upon W. Mark Crain, Randall Holcombe, and Robert D. Tollison, "Monopoly Aspects of Political Parties," *Atlantic Economic Journal* 7, no. 2 (July 1979): 54–58.

5. Gordon Tullock, "Entry Barriers in Politics," *American Economic Review* 55, no. 2 (Mar. 1965): 459.

6. Variations in the cost of acquiring the majority asset are reflected in the observed relationship between campaign spending bids for political offices and anticipated majority size. W. Mark Crain and Robert D. Tollison, in "Campaign Expenditures and Political Competition," *Journal of Law and Economics* (Apr. 1976), pp. 177–88, provide some empirical

evidence on this point using campaign expenditure data from elections for the United States House of Representatives.

7. Public Law 93-443; 93rd Congress, S. 3044, is a comprehensive campaign reform law, including the provision for public funding of presidential candidates and the campaign contribution limits. Presently there are strong pressures to extend the subsidy to all Federal elections, which is predictable within the confines of the model.

8. This may not be entirely true, since one party may have a comparative advantage through price discrimination. In American politics, it would probably be the Republican party, which has more wealthy party members, in wihch case the campaign limitations would be more likely to be passed by a Democratic congress, as was the case. Republicans still might desire the new system, however.

9. The campaign contribution limitation is typically explained as a mechanism for incumbents to keep challengers from raising funds. This explanation is subject to exceptions because incumbents can usually raise far more money than challengers, so that the law would constrain incumbents more than challengers. Another explanation for the law is that it is an attempt to internalize the externality under discussion in the text. The next section of this chapter deals explicitly with competition between incumbents and nonincumbents.

10. Robert Tollison, W. Mark Crain, and Paul Pautler, in "Information and Voting: An Empirical Note," *Public Choice* (Winter 1975), pp. 43–50, estimated some effects of information on voter turnout and found that candidates' broadcasting expenditures were not a statistically significant determinant of turnout, even at the 20 percent level of significance. One explanation of their finding is that information generated by the news media gives voters all the information that they rationally care to acquire. Although expenditures do not increase turnout, they still could affect the percentage of the vote going to a candidate.

11. W. Mark Crain, "On the Structure and Stability of Political Markets," *Journal of Political Economy* 85, no. 4 (Aug. 1977): 829–42, presents a perceptive analysis of aspects of competition between incumbents and nonincumbents.

12. In a random sample of elections to the United States House of Representatives, my former colleague Righard Higgins found that incumbents defeated nonincumbents 85 percent of the time.

13. Limitations on campaign expenditures is an example cited earlier in the chapter.

14. The next chapter deals with this issue within a contractarian framework.

15. Crain, "On the Structure and Stability of Political Markets."

16. Downs, *An Economic Theory of Democracy*, chap. 7. See chapter 2 of the present work for an exposition of Downs's model.

17. Niskanen, *Bureaucracy and Representative Government.*

18. Thompson, "Review of Niskanen's *Bureaucracy and Representative Government.*"

19. This section is a slightly modified version of Randall G. Holcombe and Edward O. Price III, "Optimality and the Institutional Structure of Bureaucracy," *Public Choice* 33, no. 1 (1978): 55–59.

20. This representation of Niskanen's model is specific to what he calls the budget constrained region.

21. Similar suggestions have been made with respect to related institutional problems before. See, for examples, Tullock, "Entry Barriers in Politics," and Harold Demsetz, "Why Regulate Utilities?" *Journal of Law and Economics* 11 (1968): 55–65.

22. See Armen A. Alchian, "Some Economics of Property Rights," *Il Politico* 30, no. 4 (1965): 816–29. Gordon Tullock, *The Politics of Bureaucracy* (Washington, D.C.: Public Affairs Press, 1965), presents an unusual model of bureaucratic inefficiency from a different perspective.

23. At some motels and restaurants, the parking concessions are leased to the highest bidder. The same is true of bell captains at some hotels. The money they make in tips pays for the lease and provides competitive wages to the employees. This is a private sector analog to selling monopoly rights to public sector bureaus and public utilities.

Chapter 8. A Contractarian Model of the State

1. See Scott Gordon, "The New Contracterians," *Journal of Political Economy* 84, no. 3 (June 1976): 573–90.

2. This chapter is based upon Randall G. Holcombe, "The Continuing Social Contract," *Social Science* 53, no. 4 (Autumn 1978): 211–16; and Randall G. Holcombe, "A Contracterian Model of the Decline in Classical Liberalism," *Public Choice* 35, no. 3 (1980): 277–86.

3. For examples, see Roger D. Blair, Paul B. Ginsberg, and Ronald J. Vogel, "Blue Cross-Blue Shield Administration Costs: A Study of Non-Profit Health Insurers," *Economic Inquiry* 13 (June 1975): 237–51, on insurance; C.M. Lindsay, "A Theory of Government Enterprise," *Journal of Political Economy* 84 (Oct. 1976): 1061–77, on hospital care costs; and D.G. Davies, "The Efficiency of Public versus Private Firms: The Case of Australia's Two Airlines," *Journal of Law and Economics* 14 (Apr. 1971): 141–65, on airlines.

4. For examples, see Alchian, "Some Economics of Property Rights," Niskanen, *Bureaucracy and Representative Government,* and Tullock, *The Politics of Bureaucracy.*

5. For examples, see E.K. Browning, "Why the Social Insurance Budget Is too Large in a Democracy," *Economic Inquiry* 13 (Sept. 1975): 373–88; Buchanan, "Politics, Policy, and the Pigouvian Margin"; and

Downs, "Why the Government Budget Is too Small in a Democracy." Other studies, such as Bowen, "The Interpretation of Voting in the Allocation of Economic Resources," Barr and Davis, "An Elementary Political and Economic Theory of the Expenditures of State and Local Governments," and Tiebout, "A Pure Theory of Local Expenditures," have emphasized the efficiency of governmental institutions. Downs, *An Economic Theory of Democracy,* and Buchanan and Tullock, *The Calculus of Consent,* provide classic treatments of conditions under which political activity could be expected to be efficient or inefficient.

6. The basic theme of these studies is that entrepreneurs will spend up to the expected value of the monopoly rent to compete for the monopoly, dissipating the entire surplus. See, for examples, Anne O. Kreuger, "The Political Economy of the Rent-Seeking Society," *American Economic Review* 64 (June 1974), pp. 291–303; Gordon Tullock, "The Welfare Costs of Tariffs, Monopolies, and Theft,"*Western Economic Journal* 4 (June 1967): 224–32; and Gordon Tullock, "The Transitional Gains Trap," *Bell Journal of Economics* 6 (Autumn 1975): 671–78.

7. Buchanan, in "Public Finance and Public Choice," has noted a major transformation in the public finance literature since World War II, with increased emphasis on the incentives of public sector decision makers.

8. Some writers have dealt either directly or indirectly with this problem. For example, Niskanen, in *Bureaucracy and Representative Government,* described the growth of a bureaucracy as the demand for its services increased, and Milton Friedman, in *Capitalism and Freedom,* noted that a free society must preserve the right of its opponents to campaign against that type of social organization. Hayek, in *The Road to Serfdom,* believed that although all members of a society share the common goal of improving the quality of the society, those advocating increasing government activity did not realize what would be the consequences of their proposals. Closer to the theme of this chapter is the suggestion by Tullock, in his review of Niskanen's *Bureaucracy and Representative Government,* that as the government gets larger, more people are employed by the government, which means that more voters desire a larger government to promote their self-interest as government employees, causing the government to grow even more.

9. One possible answer to this question is that the government is in fact not exercising more influence—that the present governmental influence has always existed. Hughes, *The Governmental Habit,* details a long history of the use of governmental influence to further private interests. Indeed the same incentives to use governmental influence to further private interests have always existed, but the size (though perhaps not the scope) of governmental activity has been expanding over

time. This chapter relies on and complements theories such as those of Hughes; Posner, in "Taxation by Regulation," *Bell Journal of Economics and Management Science* 2 (Spring 1971): 22–50; and Stigler in "The Theory of Economic Regulation," *Bell Journal of Economics and Management Science* 2 (Spring 1971): 3–21, who explain incentives for governmental influence over resource allocation. This chapter explains not why this influence exists, or when it began, but why it would be expected to grow over time in a liberal society.

10. Some related questions are addressed in James M. Buchanan and Richard E. Wagner, *Democracy in Deficit: The Political Legacy of Lord Keynes* (New York: Academic Press, 1977).

11. Sir Ernest Barker, in his introduction to *Social Contract* (New York & London: Oxford Univ. Press, 1960), traces the origin of the social contract to Plato.

12. See James M. Buchanan, *The Limits of Liberty: Between Anarchy and Leviathan* (Chicago: Univ. of Chicago Press, 1975), and John Rawls, *A Theory of Justice* (Cambridge: Harvard Univ. Press, Belknap Press, 1971).

13. Buchanan and Tullock, *The Calculus of Consent.*

14. Rawls goes beyond the mere description of the procedure for selecting of a social contract to suggest what the terms of the contract would be. D. Meuller, R. Tollison, and T. Willett, in "The Utilitarian Contract: A Generalization of Rawls's Theory of Justice," *Theory and Decision* 4 (1974): 345–67, criticize Rawls's description of the terms of the social contract. Rawls defends his use of the maximin principle in his "Some Reasons for the Maximin Criterion," *American Economic Review* 64 (May 1974): 141–46.

15. On this point, it is interesting to note Barker's statement that in England, "the house of Lords, as a part of the Convention Parliament, had agreed by 55 votes to 46 that there was an original contract between the King and the People" (*Social Contract*, p. xxii).

16. See Buchanan, *The Limits of Liberty*, p. 167.

17. Mueller, Tollison, and Willett, in "The Utilitarian Contract," criticize Rawls's description of the terms of the social contract. Rawls defends his use of his often-criticized maximin principle in "Some Reasons for the Maximin Criterion." For a more general discussion concerning the social contract, see Scott Gordon, "The New Contracterians," *Journal of Political Economy* 84 (June 1976): 573–90; and Holcombe, "The Continuing Social Contract."

18. This is not meant to imply that from the beginning the government was not used to further special interests. Indeed, the use of government as a vehicle for private gain is chronicled by Hughes's *The Governmental Habit*. Rather, this paragraph is contending that by setting up the constitution within a framework resembling Rawls's conceptual

ideas, large scale political favoritism could grow only slowly, since the constitution would have to be written in such a manner that if the writers were not elected, they could not fall victim to the political power of those who were.

19. This point is made by Kreuger and Tullock in the works referenced in note 6, above. Both of these authors suggest that the inefficiency is the result of too much governmental activity.

20. Rothbard, in *For a New Liberty,* argues against any government and in favor of an orderly anarchy because (for one reason) he asserts that an anarchistic region is more difficult for outside aggressors to take over than one in which there is a well-defined government. This model suggests the threat of internal rather than external oppression, but along similar lines. This is not to say, however, that a society would be better off under anarchy; but Rothbard provides some interesting arguments about the benefits of an orderly anarchy and gives some well-developed ideas on how such a system could be maintained.

21. This phenomenon was noted by George Simmel, in *The Philosophy of Money* (1907; reprint ed., London and Boston: Routledge and Kegan Paul, 1978), p. 298, who noted that "we are much more dependent on the whole society through the complexity of our needs on the one hand, and the specialization of our abilities on the other, . . . we are remarkably independent of every *specific* member of this society." This quotation was found in David Laidler and Nicholas Rowe, "George Simmel's *Philosophy of Money:* A Review Article for Economics," *Journal of Economic Literature* 18 (March 1980), p. 99.

Chapter 9. Economic Efficiency and the Evolution of the Common Law

1. Economists who are champions of the free market have frequently emphasized the relationship between economic and political freedom. Good examples are Milton Friedman, in *Capitalism and Freedom,* Hayek, in *The Road to Serfdom,* and Friedman and Friedman, in *Free to Choose.*

2. Hugh Thomas, *A History of the World* (New York: Harper & Row, 1979), pp. 157–58.

3. See, for instance, Richard A. Posner's *Economic Analysis of Law* (Boston Little, Brown, 1972), which argues that the law is in general efficient, but does not analyze the origins of different types of law.

4. Codifications of bodies of common law have been written. These documents are not the law, however, but the author's perception of the law as implied by court decisions.

5. Standard reading for the law student on this subject is *The Bramble Bush* (New York: Oceana Publications, 1951) by K.N. Llewellyn, especially chapter 4.

6. This is the test for negligence under the Hand formula. For a discussion, see Posner, *Economic Analysis of Law*, pp. 69–70.

7. For this reason, as noted earlier, there is little reason for economists to distinguish common from statutory law when examining the merits of a particular law in relation to a particular case.

8. There is some reason to believe that legislatures would be more prone to make inefficient laws than judges, since legislatures are frequently under pressure to (and do) pass laws to help special interest groups at the expense of the general society. Judges would tend to be more impartial and consider simply what the proper rule should be in a particular case. In addition, judges do not hear cases in which they have a personal interest in the outcome. However, the tendency for judiciary decisions to be more closely in line with the public interest than legislative rules will be disregarded here, and legislatures and courts will both be assumed equally likely to arrive at efficient laws.

9. A similar example appears in Llewellyn, *The Bramble Bush*, chap. 4.

10. I am indebted to Robert Summers for introducing me to the legal history appearing in this section.

11. W.L. Prosser, *Handbook of the Law of Torts* (4th ed., 1971), p. 139.

12. Kings Bench, 1809, 11 East 60.

13. Posner, in *Economic Analysis of Law*, p. 70, suggests that this rule is not efficient, apparently because he applies the rule in a case where he already has calculated the outcome. In the *Butterfield* example, if Forrester knew that Butterfield would be riding in a contributorily negligent manner, Forrester would have no incentive to exercise care. But since, before the fact, the possibility exists that an individual exercising ordinary care might also be injured on the pole, Forrester still has the incentive to be careful not to cause injury negligently to an individual who is exercising ordinary care. An individual could not foresee every possible injury that could occur due to his behavior, and the court, therefore, only expects him to be liable in cases where the injured individual could not have reasonably been expected to avoid the injury.

14. Exchequer, 1842, 10 M&W, 545.

15. Privy Council, 1915 [1916], 1 Appeal Cases 719. The reference to this case, unlike the earlier two, is to an appellate opinion. Loach won the original case.

16. William L. Prosser, in "Comparative Negligence" (51 Michigan L. Rev. 1953) states with regard to the doctrine of contributory negli-

gence that "No one has ever succeeded in justifying that as a policy, and no one ever will." Taken in concert with the other common law aspects of negligence, this chapter concludes that the contributory negligence doctrine establishes efficient incentive.

17. Posner, *Economic Analysis of Law*, pp. 84–88. Posner points out that the law might still be cost-effective even though it implies inefficient incentives.

18. Posner, in *Economic Analysis of Law*, suggests that the total incentive will not be correct, and that there may be either over- or underinvestment in accident prevention ((pp. 70–71). As in his example of contributory negligence, he arrives at this conclusion because he has assumed that a certain specific accident has happened and examined incentives as if the outcome of the accident could be foreseen.

19. See, for examples, Prosser, "Comparative Negligence"; Cornelius J. Peck, "The Role of the Courts and Legislatures in the Reform of Tort Law" (48 Minnesota L. Rev. 1963); and Glanville Williams, "Law Reform (Contributory Negligence) Act, 1945" (9 Modern L. Rev. 1946).

20. See Peck, "The Role of the Courts and Legislature in the Reform of Tort Law."

21. See, for examples, Maki v. Frelk (Supreme Court of Illinois, 1968, 239 N.E. 2d 445), and Li v. Yellow Cab Company of California (Supreme Court of California, 1975, 532 p. 2d. 1226).

22. See, for examples, John Prather Brown, "Toward an Economic Theory of Liability," *Journal of Legal Studies* 2 (June 1973): 323–49; and Jerry Green, "On the Optimal Structure of Liability Laws," *Bell Journal of Economics* 7 (Autumn 1976): 553–74.

23. Paul H. Rubin, "Why is the Common Law Efficient?" *Journal of Legal Studies* 6, no. 1 (Jan. 1977): 51–63.

24. George L. Priest, "The Common Law Process and the Selection of Efficient Rules," *Journal of Legal Studies* 6, no. 1 (Jan. 1977): 65–82.

25. This can be contrasted to the inquisitional system used in some European countries.

26. See, for examples, Posner, *Economic Analysis of Law*, and Gordon Tullock, *The Logic of the Law* (New York: Basic Books, 1971).

27. While the specific process of the development of the common law has not been examined, many writers have examined the emergence of efficient and/or just social rules. Some recent examples are James M. Buchanan, *The Limits of Liberty;* Robert Nozick, *Anarchy, State, and Utopia* (New York: Basic Books, 1974); and Rawls, *A Theory of Justice.*

28. This phrase is taken from the title to chapter 6 of *Studies in Philosophy, Politics and Economics* (New York: Simon and Schuster, 1967), by F.A. Hayek. The general theme of this chapter—that the law evolves as a result of human action, but not of human design—is presented in

Hayek's *Law, Legislation, and Liberty,* vol. 1 (Chicago: Univ. of Chicago Press, 1973). Hayek traces the idea to many earlier thinkers. The efficient development of the common law via the use of precedent in the courts is not examined in detail, although a general theme in much of Hayek's work is the ability of "spontaneous" order to produce efficiency. This principle when applied to society, is sometimes referred to as social Darwinism, although the principle far predates Darwin. Mandeville and Hume are two early thinkers in this tradition. The most thorough application of the theory of evolution to the production of order was undertaken by Herbert Spencer, whose *Synthetic Philosophy* (ten volumes) organized such diverse areas as biology, sociology, religion, psychology, and ethics under the principle of natural selection.

Chapter 10.
The Democratic Decision-making Process

1. This phrase is the title of chapter 6 of Hayek's *Studies in Philosophy, Politics and Economics.* Hayek notes that the concept goes back at least to Adam Ferguson, who published the observation in 1767.

2. The concept predates Darwin, and was articulated by David Hume.

3. See, for example, Armen A. Alchian, "Uncertainty, Evolution, and Economic Theory," *Journal of Political Economy* 58 (1950): 211–21.

4. These are the only legitimate functions of government, according to Rand, *The Virtue of Selfishness,* chap. 14. See, however, Robert Nozick, in *Anarchy, State, and Utopia,* for a theory of government provision of other outputs; and Rothbard, in *For a New Liberty,* who argues that private enterprise can successfully replace all government output.

5. This theme was developed by Hayek, *The Road to Serfdom,* and by David Friedman, "Many, Few, One: Social Harmony and the Shrunken Social Choice Set."

6. This is not true for all hypothetical election schemes, though. An alternative is the system suggested by Tideman and Tullock, "A New and Superior Process for Making Social Choices."

BIBLIOGRAPHY

Alchian, Armen A. "Some Economics of Property Rights." *Il Politico* 30, no. 4 (1965): 816–29.

———."Uncertainty, Evolution, and Economic Theory." *Journal of Political Economy* 58 (1950): 211–21.

Arrow, Kenneth J. *Social Choice and Individual Values.* 2nd ed. New Haven and London: Yale Univ. Press, 1963.

Barker, Sir Earnest. *Social Contract.* New York & London: Oxford Univ. Press, 1960.

Barlow, Robin. "Efficiency Aspects of Local School Finance." *Journal of Political Economy* 78 (Sept.–Oct. 1970): 1028–40.

———."Efficiency Aspects of Local School Finance: Reply." *Journal of Political Economy* 81 (Jan.–Feb. 1973): 192–202.

Barr, James L., and Otto A. Davis. "An Elementary Political and Economic Theory of the Expenditures and State and Local Governments," *Southern Economic Journal* 33 Oct. 1966): 149–65.

Bator, Francis M. "The Anatomy of Market Failure." *Quarterly Journal of Economics* 72 (Aug. 1958): 351–79.

Bergstrom, Theodore C., and Robert Goodman, "Private Demand for Public Goods." *American Economic Review* 63 (June 1973): 280–96.

Black, Duncan. *The Theory of Committees and Elections.* Cambridge: Cambridge Univ. Press, 1958.

Blair, Roger D., Paul B. Ginsberg, and Ronald J. Vogel. "Blue Cross-Blue Shield Administration Costs: A Study of Non-Profit Health Insurers." *Economic Inquiry* 13 (June 1975): 237–51.

Borcherding, Thomas E., and Robert T. Deacon. "The Demand for Services of Non-Federal Governments." *American Economic Review* 62 (Dec. 1972): 891–901.

Bowen, Howard R. "The Interpretation of Voting in the Allocation of Economic Resources." *Quarterly Journal of Economics* 58 (Nov. 1943): 27–48.

Bronfenbrenner, Martin. "A Percentage Budget for Public Appropriations." *National Tax Journal* 18 (Dec. 1965): 375–79.

Browning, Edgar K. "Why the Social Insurance Budget Is too large in a Democracy." *Economic Inquiry* 13 (Sept. 1975): 373–88.

Buchanan, James M. *The Demand and Supply of Public Goods.* Chicago: Rand McNally, 1968.

———."The Economics of Earmarked Taxes." *Journal of Political Economy 71 (Oct. 1963): 457–69.*

———."*An Economic Theory of Clubs.*" *Economica* (Feb. 1965), pp. 1–14.

———.*Freedom in Constitutional Contract.* College Station: Texas A & M Univ. Press, 1977.

———.*The Limits of Liberty: Between Anarchy and Leviathan.* Chicago: Univ. of Chicago Press, 1975.

———."Notes for an Economic Theory of Socialism." *Public Choice* 8 (Spring 1970): 29–43.

———."Politics, Policy, and the Pigouvian Margins." *Economica* n.s. 29 (Feb. 1962): 17–28.

———.*Public Finance and Democratic Process.* Chapel Hill: Univ. of North Carolina Press, 1967.

———."Public Finance and Public Choice." *National Tax Journal* 28 (Dec. 1975): 383–94.

———."The Relevance of Pareto Optimality." *Journal of Conflict Resolution* (Nov. 1962), pp. 341–54.

Buchanan, James M., and Marilyn Flowers. "An Analytic Setting for a Taxpayers' Revolution." *Western Economic Journal* 7 (Dec. 1969): 349–59.

Buchanan, James M., and Charles J. Goetz. "Efficiency Limits of Fiscal Mobility: An Assessment of the Tiebout Model." *Journal of Public Economics* 1 (1972): 25–43.

Buchanan, James M., and Gordon Tullock. *The Calculus of Consent.* Ann Arbor: Univ. of Michigan Press, 1962.

Buchanan, James M., and Richard E. Wagner. *Democracy in Deficit: The Political Legacy of Lord Keynes.* New York: Academic Press, 1977.

Clarke, Edward H. "Multipart Pricing of Public Goods." *Public Choice* 2 (Fall 1971): 17–33.

Crain, W. Mark. "On the Structure and Stability of Political Markets." *Journal of Political Economy* 85, no. 4 (Aug. 1977): 829–42.

Crain, W. Mark, Randall Holcombe, and Robert D. Tollison. "Monopoly Aspects of Political Parties." *Atlantic Economic Journal* 7, no. 2 (July 1979): 54–58.

Davies, David G. "The Efficiency of Public versus Private Firms: The Case of Australia's Two Airlines." *Journal of Law and Economics* 14 (Apr. 1971): 149–65.

Demsetz, Harold. "Why Regulate Utilities?" *Journal of law and Economics* 2 (1968): 55–65.

Denzau, Arthur T., and Robert J. Mackay. "Benefit Shares and Majority Voting." *American Economic Review* 66 (Mar. 1976): 69–76.

Downs, Anthony. *An Economic Theory of Democracy.* New York: Harper and Row, 1957.

————."Why the Government Budget Is too Small in a Democracy." *World Politics* 12 (July 1960): 541–64.

Friedman, David. "Many, Few, One: Social Harmony and the Shrunken Choice Set." *American Economic Review* 70, no. 1 (Mar. 1980): 225–32.

Friedman, Milton, *Capitalism and Freedom.* Chicago: Univ. of Chicago Press, 1962.

Friedman, Milton, and Rose Friedman. *Free to Choose.* New York: Harcourt Brace Jovanovich, 1980.

Gordon, Scott. "The New Contractarians." *Journal of Political Economy* 84, no. 3 (June 1976): 573–90.

Groves, Theodore. "Incentives in Teams." *Econometrica* 41 (July 1973): 617–33.

Hayek, Friedrich A. *The Road to Serfdom.* London: George Routledge & Sons, 1944.

————.*Studies in Philosophy, Politics and Economics.* New York: Simon and Schuster, 1967.

Hicks, J.R. *Value and Capital.* 2nd ed. Oxford: Oxford Univ. Press, 1946.

Holcombe, Randall G. "Concepts of Public Sector Equilibrium." *National Tax Journal* 33, no. 1 (Mar. 1980): 77–88.

————."The Continuing Social Contract." *Social Science* 53, no. 4 (Autumn 1978): 211–16.

————."A Contractarian Model of the Decline in Classical Liberalism." *Public Choice* 35, no. 3 (1980): 260–74.

————."An Empirical Test of the Median Voter Model." *Economic Inquiry* 18, no. 2 (Apr. 1980): 260–74.

————."The Florida System: A Bowen Equilibrium Referendum Process." *National Tax Journal* 30 (Mar. 1977): 77–84.

_____."A Public Choice Analysis of Millage Issue Elections for Financing Public Schools." Ph.D. diss., Virginia Polytechnic Institute and State University, 1975.

_____."Public Choice and Public Spending." *National Tax Journal* 31 (Dec. 1978): 373–83.

Holcombe, Randall G., and Edward O. Price III. "Optimality and the Institutional Structure of Bureaucracy." *Public Choice* 33, no. 1 (Spring 1978): 55–59.

Holcombe, Randall G., and Paul C. Taylor. "Tax Referenda and the Voluntary Exchange Model of Taxation." *Public Finance Quarterly* 8, no. 1 (Jan. 1980): 107–14.

Hotelling, Harold. "Stability in Competition." *Economic Journal* 39 (Mar. 1929): 41–57.

Hughes, Jonathan R. T. *The Governmental Habit.* New York: Basic Books, 1977.

Inman, Robert P. "Testing Political Economy's 'as if' Assumption: Is the Median Income Voter Really Decisive?" *Public Choice* 33, no. 4 (1978): 45–65.

Jackson, Raymond. "A 'Taxpayers' Revolution' and Economic Rationality." *Public Choice* 10 (Spring 1971): 93–96.

Keynes, John Maynard. *The General Theory of Employment, Interest and Money.* New York: Harcourt, Brace, 1936.

Kreuger, Anne O. "The Political Economy of the Rent-Seeking Society." *American Economic Review* 64 (June 1974): 291–303.

Laidler, David, and Nicholas Rowe, "George Simmel's *Philosophy of Money:* A Review Article for Economists." *Journal of Economic Literature* 18 (Mar. 1980): 97–105.

Lindahl, Erik. "Just Taxation—A Positive Solution" (1919). In Richard A. Musgrave and Alan T. Peacock, eds., *Classics in the Theory of Public Finance.* New York: St. Martin's Press, 1967. Pp. 168–76.

Lindsay, Cotton M. "A Theory of Government Enterprise." *Journal of Political Economy* 84 (Oct. 1976): 1061–77.

McEachern, William A. "Collective Decision Rules and Local Debt Choice: A test of the Median-Voter Hypothesis." *National Tax Journal* 31, no. 2 (June 1978): 129–36.

Mackay, Robert J., and Carolyn L. Weaver. "Monopoly Bureaus and Fiscal Outcomes: Deductive Models and Implications for Reform." In Gordon Tullock and Richard E. Wagner, eds., *Policy Analysis and De-*

ductive Reasoning. Lexington, Mass.: D. C. Heath, Lexington Books, 1978. Pp. 141–65.

Mueller, D., R. Tollison, and T. Willett. "The Utilitarian Contract: A Generalization of Rawls' Theory of Justice." *Theory and Decision* 4 (1974): 345–67.

Musgrave, Richard A. *The Theory of Public Finance.* New York: McGraw-Hill, 1959.

Niskanen, William A. *Bureaucracy and Representative Government.* Chicago and New York: Aldine-Atherton, 1971.

————."Bureaucrats and Politicians." *Journal of Law and Economics* 18 (Dec. 1975): 617–43.

————."The Peculiar Economics of Bureaucracy." *American Economic Review* 58 (May 1968): 293–305.

Nozick, Robert. *Anarchy, State, and Utopia.* New York: Basic Books, 1974.

Pigou, A.C. *The Economics of Welfare.* 4th ed. London: MacMillan, 1932.

Plott, Charles R., and Michael E. Levine. "A Model of Agenda Influence on Committee Decisions." *American Economic Review* 68, no. 1 (Mar. 1978): 146–60.

Posner, Richard A. "Taxation by Regulation." *Bell Journal of Economics and Management Science* 2 (Spring 1971): 22–50.

Rand, Ayn. *The Virtue of Selfishness.* New York: New American Library, 1961.

Rawls, John. "Some Reasons for the Maximum Criterion." *American Economic Review* 64 (May 1974): 141–46.

————.*A Theory of Justice.* Cambridge: Harvard Univ. Press, Belknap Press, 1971.

Romer, Thomas, and Howard Rosenthal. "Bureaucrats Versus Voters: On the Political Economy of Resource Allocation by Direct Democracy." *Quarterly Journal of Economics* 93, no. 4 (Nov. 1979): 563–87.

————."Political Resource Allocation, Controlled Agendas, and the Status Quo." *Public Choice* 33, no. 4 (1978): 27–43.

Rothbard, Murray N. *For a New Liberty.* New York: Macmillan, 1973.

Samuelson, Paul A. "A Diagrammatic Exposition of a Theory of Public Expenditure." *Review of Economics and Statistics* 37 (Nov. 1955): 350–56.

————."The Pure Theory of Public Expenditure," *Review of Economics and Statistics* 36 (Nov. 1954): 387–89.

Simmel, George. *The Philosophy of Money.* 1907. Reprinted. London and Boston: Routledge and Kegan Paul, 1978.

Smith, Adam. *The Wealth of Nations.* New York: Random House, Modern Library, 1937.

Stigler, George J. "Director's Law of Public Income Redistribution." *Journal of Law and Economics* 13 (Apr. 1970): 1–10.

_____."The Theory of Economic Regulation." *Bell Journal of Economics and Management Science* 2 (Spring 1971): 3–21.

Thompson, Earl A. "A Pareto-Optimal Group Decision Process," *Papers on Nonmarket Decision Making* 1 (1965): 133–40.

_____."Review of Niskanen's *Bureaucracy and Representative Government.*" *Journal of Economic Literature* 11 (Sept. 1973): 950–53.

Tideman, T. Nicolaus. "The Capabilities of Voting Rules in the Absence of Coalitions." In T. N. Clark, ed., *Citizen Preferences and Urban Public Policy.* Beverly Hills: Sage Publications, 1976. Pp. 23–44.

Tideman, T. Nicolaus, and Gordon Tullock. "A New and Superior Process for Making Social Choices." *Journal of Political Economy* 84 (Dec. 1976): 1145–60.

Tiebout, Charles M. "A Pure Theory of Local Expenditures." *Journal of Political Economy* 64 (Oct. 1956): 416–24.

Tollison, Robert, W. Mark Crain, and Paul Pantler. "Information and Voting: An Empirical Note." *Public Choice* (Winter 1975), Pp. 43–50.

Tullock, Gordon. "Entry Barriers in Politics." *American Economic Review* 55, no. 2 (Mar. 1965): 458–66.

_____.*The Politics of Bureaucracy.* Washington, D.C.: Public Affairs Press, 1965.

_____."Review of Niskanen's *Bureaucracy and Representative Government.*" *Public Chioce* 11 (Spring 1972): 119–24.

_____."The Transitional Gains Trap." *Bell Journal of Economics* 6 (Autumn 1975): 671–78.

_____."The Welfare Costs of Tariffs, Monopolies, and Theft." *Western Economic Journal* 4 (June 1967): 224–32.

Wicksell, Knut. "A New Principle of Just Taxation" (1896). In Richard A. Musgrave and Alan T. Peacock, eds., *Classics in the Theory of Public Finance.* New York: St. Martin's Press, 1967. Pp. 72–118.

INDEX

Randall G. Holcombe is on the faculty of the Department of Economics at Auburn University, where he has taught since 1977. He has also been on the faculty of Texas A & M University. His journal articles have been published in *Economic Inquiry, Journal of Public Economics, National Tax Journal, Public Choice, Public Finance Quarterly,* and *Southern Economic Journal.*